SATANISM

Zondervan
Guide to Cults &
Religious Movements

First Series

Second Series

ZONDERVAN
GUIDE to CULTS &
RELIGIOUS
MOVEMENTS

SATANISM

BOB AND GRETCHEN PASSANTINO
Authors

Alan W. Gomes
Series Editor

ZONDERVAN™

GRAND RAPIDS, MICHIGAN 49530 USA

To Dr. Walter R. Martin (1928–1989)

A personal friend, teacher, and mentor who wrote the first Zondervan series on cults (1950s). He taught us never to give up and to contend earnestly for the faith once for all entrusted to the saints (Jude 3).

ZONDERVAN™

Satanism
Copyright © 1995 by Bob and Gretchen Passantino, dba, G. P. Publisher Services

Requests for information should be addressed to:

Zondervan, *Grand Rapids, Michigan 49530*

Library of Congress Cataloging-in-Publication Data

Passantino, Robert.
　　Satanism / Bob and Gretchen Passantino.
　　　　p.　cm. — (Zondervan guide to cults and religious movements)
　　Includes bibliographical references.
　　ISBN: 0-310-70451-0 (softcover)
　　1. Satanism—Controversial literature.　2. Satanism—United States—Controversial literature.　I. Passantino, Gretchen.　II. Title.　III. Series.
　　BF1548.P37　1995
　　133.4'22—dc20　　　　　　　　　　　　　　　　　　　　　95-8262
　　　　　　　　　　　　　　　　　　　　　　　　　　　　　　CIP

Edited by James E. Ruark
Interior design by Art Jacobs

Printed in the United States of America

03　04　05　06　07　08 09　/ ❖ CH /　12　11　10　9　8　7　6　5　4　3

Contents

How to Use This Book

The *Zondervan Guide to Cults and Religious Movements* comprises sixteen volumes, treating many of the most important groups and belief systems confronting the Christian church today. This series distills the most important facts about each and presents a well-reasoned, cogent Christian response. The authors in this series are highly qualified, well-respected professional Christian apologists with considerable expertise on their topics.

For ease of use we have sought to maintain the same "look and feel" for all the books. We designed the structure and layout to help you find the information you need as quickly as possible.

All the volumes are written in outline form. Each book contains an introduction to the cult, movement, or belief system. The theology section is arranged by doctrinal topic, such as God, Christ, sin, and salvation. The movement's position on each topic is set forth objectively, primarily from its own official writings. The group's teachings are then refuted point by point, followed by an affirmative presentation of what the Bible says about the doctrine. Following the theology section is a discussion of witnessing tips. While each witnessing encounter must be handled individually and sensitively, this section provides some helpful general guidelines, including both dos and don'ts. The books also have annotated bibliographies, listing works by the groups themselves as well as books written by Christians in response. Each book concludes with a parallel comparison chart. Arranged topically, the chart juxtaposes direct quotations from the cultic literature in the left column with the biblical refutation on the right. This volume also contains a glossary that will help to clarify difficult or misunderstood terms.

One potential problem with a detailed outline is that it is easy to lose one's place in the overall structure. To overcome this problem we have provided graphical "signposts" at the top of the odd-numbered pages. Functioning like a "you are here" map in a shopping mall, these graphics show your place in the outline, including the sections that come before and after your current position. In the theology section we have also used "icons" in the margins to make clear at a glance whether the material is being presented from the cultic or Christian viewpoint. A striking feature of this volume on Satanism is that in conducting their research, the authors interviewed Anton Szandor LaVey, founder of the Church of Satan. LaVey stated that this interview, conducted 5 August 1994, is the first he has granted for publication in fifteen years.

We hope you will find these books useful as you seek "to give an answer to everyone who asks you to give the reason for the hope that you have" (1 Peter 3:15).

—Alan W. Gomes, Ph.D.
Series Editor

 # Part I: Introduction

A glow of new light is borne out of the night and Lucifer is risen, once more to proclaim: "This is the age of Satan! Satan Rules the Earth!" (Anton Szandor LaVey, *The Satanic Bible*, 23).

[God] having disarmed the powers and authorities, he made a public spectacle of them, triumphing over them by the cross (*The Holy Bible*, Col. 2:15).

I. What Is Satanism?

A. The Difficulty of Classifying Satanists

1. Contemporary satanists defy easy classification. This is partly because of the independent nature of satanism and partly because of satanists' desire for secrecy.

2. If satanists could be characterized in one term, it would be "self-serving." That is, one's own needs, desires, beliefs, and goals are supreme. Consequently, it is to be expected that *satanism* could have almost as many definitions as practitioners.

B. The Worship of "Satan" the Common Factor

1. "Contemporary satanism is a form of religious belief and expression holding to the worship of Satan, whether Satan is defined as a supernatural person, a deity, a devil, a supernatural force, a natural force, an innate human force, or, most commonly, the self."[1]

2. Most satanists, such as Church of Satan founder Anton Szandor LaVey, are strict materialistic iconoclasts who worship themselves[2] and use the term "Satan" to symbolize their rejection of Christianity, which they define as self-sacrificing, self-debasing, self-denying, oppressive, and powerless. These satanists do not believe in the existence of any spiritual being, Satan or God; they believe in the power of the self.

3. Some satanists (usually self-styled teenage satanists who make up their own system) are not sure whether either God or Satan exists,

---

[1] Bob Passantino and Gretchen Passantino, *When the Devil Dares Your Kids* (Ann Arbor, Mich.: Servant Books, 1991), 34. See also Arthur Lyons, *Satan Wants You: The Cult of Devil Worship in America* (New York: Mysterious Press, 1988), 9.

[2] "We don't worship Satan, we worship ourselves using the metaphorical representation of the qualities of Satan" (quoted by Blanche Barton, *The Secret Life of a Satanist. The Authorized Biography of Anton LaVey* [Los Angeles: Feral House, 1990], 205).

but they practice their system as though Satan were a powerful spirit being who can give the worshiper power for self-indulgence. These satanists would agree that "Whatever the truth is, this works."

4. Some satanists believe that spiritual power exists, but this power is not directed by any personal entities, spirit or material. This power is available to anyone who learns how to harness it. These satanists practice using this power for self-advancement, not for selfless acts of goodness toward others.

5. Some satanists believe that competing, equal spiritual forces exist (whether personal—God and Satan, or impersonal—good and bad), either of which can be used by humans to achieve power goals. This religious view is known as a form of *dualism*. These satanists have chosen to use the negative, destructive, or self-indulgent spiritual force.

6. A few satanists (usually self-styled teenage satanists or mentally aberrant adults) believe what the Bible says about God and Satan, but have chosen allegiance to Satan in this life even though they believe that thereby they may be condemned to eternal punishment after death.

C. Satan as Defined in the Bible

1. The Hebrew word from which we get the English term *Satan* comes from a root that means one who opposes or accuses.[3] While the Greek sometimes transliterates the Hebrew term, forming *satanas* (Mark 1:13; Luke 22:3), the corresponding Greek term is *diabolos* (John 6:70; 8:44), and the English term is *devil*.[4]

2. In addition to being used as the name of the chief fallen angel (Luke 10:18), the Hebrew term is used in the Bible to refer (a) to a human opponent, as in 2 Samuel 19:22; (b) as one sent by God to block one's way, as in Numbers 22:22; and (c) as an *evil* adversary, as in Zechariah 3:1–2.

3. *Demon*, from the Greek *daimon*, or "spiritual power," is often popularly synonymous with devil (Greek version of Isa. 65:11; Matt. 8:31).

4. Other less frequently used terms include *Beelzebul*[5] (Matt. 10:25), "the evil one" (Matt. 5:37), and one of the evil or unclean spirits (Matt. 12:45; Mark 6:7).

---

[3]H. Bietenhard, "Satan," in *The New International Dictionary of New Testament Theology*, ed. Colin Brown (Grand Rapids: Zondervan, 1978), 3:486.

[4]Ibid., 450–51.

[5]The definition of Beelzebul (sometimes rendered Beelzebub) is unclear. The Hebrew perhaps refers to the "Lord of the Flies," or "the lord of the idol-sacrifice" and the Greek to the "chief demon" (see Brown, *NIDNTT*, 3:469, 472–73).

II. Statistics Regarding Contemporary Satanism

Because satanism is largely a solitary, secretive, and self-oriented religion, accurate, precise statistics are impossible to obtain.[6] However, we can give general information about proportionate participation.

A. *The False Rumors of Widespread Conspiracies*

1. It is not true that there are millions of secret satanists participating in a widespread, nearly invincible, nearly undetectable conspiracy reaching into the highest levels of church, government, law enforcement, and education. Such conspiracy theories are sensationalistic, undocumented, and propagation of such theories is irresponsible. Additionally, they are generally presented within a worldview that attributes more power to Satan and his workers than does the Bible.[7]

2. There are three main reasons for the continuing popularity of this myth.

   a. Well-meaning Christians fail to test such a rumor since it seems to be compatible with a biblical interpretation concerning the rise of false belief in the last days. (The Bible nowhere says that such a rise in false belief will be nearly invincible or undetectable.)

   b. Public satanists such as LaVey and Temple of Set founder Michael Aquino may allow higher statistics to be attributed to their groups as pseudo-evidence of the power and popularity of their churches.[8]

   c. Secular media and others substitute ratings-building sensationalism for careful journalistic investigation.

B. *What Satanism Is Not*

Contemporary satanism is not a harmless pastime of "losers" who are already disaffected from society.

1. It is not true that only psychotic serial killers, suicidal teenagers, or losers "fall" for satanism and therefore it can be dismissed as a self-defeating social anomaly.

---

[6]When we use the term *satanism* in this volume, we are referring specifically to those who dedicate themselves to the worship of Satan, however they define "Satan." While any and all forms of opposition to Christianity and any and all pagan, polytheistic religions are diametrically opposed to biblical faith and in that sense are "satanic," they are not the religious system that is the focus of this volume.

[7]Some of the sensational books that advocate the conspiracy theory are *The Secret Diary of a Satan Worshipper* by Joel French (Green Forest, Ark.: New Leaf Press, 1991); *The Edge of Evil* by Jerry Johnston (Dallas: Word, 1989); *Satan's Underground* by Lauren Stratford (Eugene, Oreg.: Harvest House, 1988); *The Satan Seller* by Mike Warnke (Plainfield, N.J.: Logos, 1972); and *Schemes of Satan* by Mike Warnke (Tulsa: Victory House, 1991). We do not recommend any of these books because they variously contain sensational, erroneous, or unreliable information and argumentation.

[8]For example, LaVey's church grants lifetime memberships, so anyone who was ever a member of the Church of Satan is counted in current statistics (Shawn Carlson and Gerald Larue, eds., *Satanism in America* [El Cerrito, Calif.: Gaia Press, 1989], 22). Additionally, the Church of Satan does not publish its own statistics because, according to LaVey, "If it's too low, we would be perceived as insignificant, and if it was too high we'd be considered too much of a threat and there would be reason to destroy us. If you can be quantified, then you can be expendable, then you can be disposed of" (quoted in Barton, *The Secret Life of a Satanist*, 202).

    2. Public satanists such as LaVey and Aquino promote a religious self-indulgence that appeals to many who have rejected Christianity and are looking for self-fulfillment.

    3. While the number of teenagers who practice self-styled satanism for more than a few months or years is small, those who at least dabble in self-styled satanism are numerous and their activities and beliefs frequently affect others.

    4. From a Christian perspective, whether few or many worship Satan, and whether few or many are mentally unsound, anyone who worships Satan (however defined and for however long) needs the life-transforming gospel of Jesus Christ.

C. *Evidence for the Prevalence of Satanism*

    1. While precise statistics are inherently unobtainable, the consensus of careful researchers is that the total number of people who would describe themselves as satanists is somewhat fewer than 6,000 worldwide.[9]

    2. The vast majority of satanists are self-styled (i.e., they put together their own system).

      a. Most self-styled satanists practice their faith alone or with a small group (many times no more than twelve others).

      b. These small groups generally exist for a few months or so.

      c. Very few last longer, and those that do generally join a public satanic church such as LaVey's Church of Satan.

    3. Of the public satanic churches, LaVey's Church of Satan is the most well-known, followed by Aquino's Temple of Set and then other small groups that have managed to garner some media attention.[10]

    4. Smaller satanic groups include the Church of Satanic Brotherhood, Ordo Templi Satanas, Order of the Black Ram, Shrine of the Little Mother, Church of S.A.T.A.N.,[11] Thee Church of Satan, Order of Baal, the Satanic Church, Thee Orthodox Satanic Church, and the Church of Satanic Liberation.[12]

    5. Mail-order catalog and newsletter lists provide some continuity among most satanists, as do the books of LaVey such as *The Satanic Bible* and *The Satanic Rituals*.

---

[9]Passantino and Passantino, *When the Devil Dares Your Kids*, 211; Lyons, *Satan Wants You*, 14.

[10]LaVey disdains the offshoots as less than serious, saying, "They serve as filters, drawing off the creeps, crumb-bums and air-heads" (Interview, 5 August 1994).

[11]In this title, "S.A.T.A.N." does not form an acronym. The form of the title avoids trademark infringement with LaVey's church.

[12]See Barton, *The Secret Life of a Satanist*, 127.

D. Generalizations Derived from Satanic Demographics

1. Most satanists are male.
2. Most are young (ages thirteen to thirty).
3. Most practice their satanism privately and live in the "real" world of employment and normal social relationships most of the time.
4. Most view Christianity or any other traditional religion as narrow, defeatist, self-abasing, and devoid of power.[13]
5. Most view traditional ethical norms as depriving the individual of self-gratification and as denying the "rights" of the individual for the "rights" of the society.
6. Most, like LaVey, practice satanism because it appears to "work" for them.[14] LaVey attributes the success of satanism to this appeal to pragmatism: "It makes sense, therefore it might enrich their lives."[15]

---

[13]Ibid., 178.
[14]Interview, 5 August 1994.
[15]Ibid.

 **Part II:** *History*

I. Introduction

A. *The Scope of This Study*

1. Throughout history there have been those who oppose the true God of the Bible, whose allegiances belong to antichrists instead of the Lord.

2. Today, as before, some people who reject the truth of the gospel set themselves up as adversaries to Christianity. (Satan is called the "enemy" in 1 Peter 5:8.)

3. In our contemporary pluralistic society, where Christian faith is at best tolerated and usually mocked, some adversaries openly feel free to call themselves *satanists.*

B. *Two Perspectives from Which the History of Satanism May Be Viewed*

1. When satanism is defined broadly to include any and all kinds of opposition to the only true God of the Bible, it encompasses many kinds of religious beliefs, actions, and movements. This definition is not the one we have described above (see Part I, Section I.A–B).

2. Using the more focused definition (satanism as the worship of "Satan," however the term "Satan" is defined), we can trace historically particular beliefs, practices, and worship regarding *Satan,* the one named in the Bible as the chief evil spirit, and then the further beliefs that provide the foundation for contemporary satanism. This is the focus of this book.

II. The Bible and Satan[16]

The Bible's focus is on God and his relationship to man, and consequently angels and demons are almost incidentally mentioned. There are few explicit Scriptures regarding Satan and other demons and a comprehensive, systematic demonology did not develop within the biblical period of history.[17]

A. *General Biblical References to Satan and Demons*

1. The Old Testament first mentions the person we know as Satan in Genesis 3:1–4, where he is pictured as a serpent "more crafty than any

---

[16]Additional Scripture and commentary on Satan are included in the theological and the comparison chart sections of this book.

[17]G. H. Twelftree, "Demon, Devil, Satan" in the *Dictionary of Jesus and the Gospels,* ed. Joel B. Green and Scot McKnight (Downers Grove, Ill.: InterVarsity Press, 1992), 163.

of the wild animals the Lord God had made." He was the instrument of Adam and Eve's temptation into sin, although God held them personally responsible for their disobedience (Gen. 3:16–19).

2. God promised that the power of Satan would be crushed by the coming Messiah: "And I will put enmity between you and the woman, and between your offspring and hers; he will crush your head, and you will strike his heel" (Gen. 3:15). This was fulfilled in the Atonement, Christ's death on the cross on our behalf (Col. 2:15).

3. Most theologians agree that the Bible identifies Satan as an angel, created by God (Ps. 148:2, 5; Col. 1:16). Evidently a certain number of angels (Jude 6) rebelled against God's authority sometime before the fall of Adam and Eve, since Satan was already evil by the time he tempted Eve to sin (Gen. 3:1–5ff.).

4. Satan's fall (whether viewed as timed from his initial rebellion or later on at the hands of the Messiah) is referred to by Christ in Luke 10:18: "I saw Satan fall like lightning from heaven." There may also be metaphorical reference to this fall in Isaiah 14:12–15 and Ezekiel 28:14–19.

5. Satan is referred to as the chief of these fallen angels, or demons, in passages such as Revelation 12:7–17 and Matthew 25:41. He is called the original liar (John 8:44) and the one who accuses the righteous (Job 1:6–12; Rev. 12:10). He is also referred to as a ruler of this wicked world and evil spiritual forces (Eph. 2:2; 6:12; John 14:30).

6. The ultimate destination of Satan and his demons is the lake of fire (Matt. 25:41; Rev. 20:10).

B. *The Bible and Angels*

1. According to Hebrews 1:13–14, angels are spiritual beings, without materiality (Num. 22:22–31), although they can assume materiality for a specific earthly purpose assigned by God (Gen. 18:2–8).

2. According to Jesus in Matthew 22:30 they are sexless, although they are capable of emotion (Luke 15:10) and are sometimes used by God in an interactive way with human beings (1 Peter 1:12).

3. They are immortal (although created, they will never cease to exist—Luke 20:36). Though confirmed in holiness, they were at one time capable of sin (Matt. 25:41).

4. The Greek *angelos* means "messenger" and with its Hebrew equivalent can mean either a human or heavenly messenger.[18] In the New Testament, *angelos* is used primarily to refer to heavenly messengers. Occasionally the term "angel of the Lord" seems to refer to God himself (Judg. 13:2ff.).

---

[18]Everret F. Harrison, ed., *Baker's Dictionary of Theology* (Grand Rapids: Baker, 1960), 41.

5. Passages such as Isaiah 6:1–3 and 1 Thessalonians 4:16 seem to imply that angels are organized in ranks or orders with specific functions in obedience to God.

6. Angels minister on God's behalf toward Christ, toward believers, and toward unbelievers.

   a. Angels operated in announcing Christ's conception (Matt. 1:20–21), in announcing his birth (Luke 2:10–12), in sustaining him during his temptation in the wilderness (Matt. 4:11) and in the Garden (Luke 22:43), in testifying to his resurrection (Matt. 28:5–7; 1 Tim. 3:16), at his ascension into heaven (Acts 1:9–11), and at his final return in glory and judgment (1 Thess. 4:16).

   b. Angels' ministry toward believers includes guidance (Gen. 24:7, 40), support (1 Kings 19:5–8), protection (Ps. 34:7), deliverance (Dan. 6:22; Acts 12:7–11), and comfort (Acts 27:23–24).

   c. Angels' responsibilities toward unbelievers involve destruction (Gen. 19:1–13), cursing (Judg. 5:23), affliction (2 Sam. 24:15–17), and persecution (Ps. 34:5–6).

C. *Power Ascribed to Satan and Other Demons in the Bible*

1. Satan and other demons have limited power in this world (Mark 3:22–30), but more power over unbelievers than over believers.

2. Concerning Nonbelievers

   Demons evidently, under certain circumstances, can control (1 John 3:10; John 8:44), invade (Luke 22:3), blind spiritually (2 Cor. 4:4), deceive (Rev. 20:7–8), and trap (1 Tim. 3:7) nonbelievers.

3. Concerning Believers

   a. Demons evidently, under certain circumstances, can tempt (1 Chron. 21:1), harass or afflict (Job 2:7), oppose (Zech. 3:1), and deceive (2 Cor. 11:3) Christians. They can also disguise demonic works as godly (2 Cor. 11:4–15).

   b. Demons *cannot* control Christians against their will because of the indwelling presence of the Holy Spirit (Matt. 12:39–45).

4. Demons cannot send anyone (believer or unbeliever) to hell (Matt. 10:28).

5. Scripture teaches that the power of Satan has been overcome by the power of the Lord Jesus Christ (Col. 2:15). Because of this, Christians have the power to resist the forces of the demonic.

   a. The Christian is to beware of Satan's trickery (2 Cor. 2:10–11).

   b. The Christian fights against demonic power with the power of the Lord and his Word (Eph. 6:11–16).

   c. The Christian can and should resist the temptations of the Devil (James 4:7; 1 Peter 5:9).

15

    d. The Christian is assured that through the power of Christ's sacrifice on the cross, Satan has been overcome (1 John 2:13; Rev. 12:10–11).

6. Both the Old and New Testaments depict people who have been controlled, deceived, afflicted, and influenced by demons or who have demonstrated unrighteousness and unbelief by partaking in the same kinds of rebellious acts as do demons. Also, the Bible attributes the source of false gods' powers as demonic.

7. The Bible does not mention any individual or group that particularly, deliberately, and knowingly worships Satan as he is identified and described in Scripture. That kind of satanism is more characteristic of the contemporary world and of some periods in history after biblical times.

III. Early Christian History (A.D. 100–400)

The church developed teaching on Satan and demons over several centuries. Developing a demonology or diabology was secondary to establishing the church, preaching the gospel, and surviving persecution.[19]

A. The early church was not dogmatic or unified on the identity of demons.

1. The church never conclusively and universally affirmed that fallen angels and demons are one and the same.[20]

2. By the end of the New Testament period and moving into the time of the apostolic fathers, most Christian writers assumed demons and fallen angels were synonymous.

B. The early church required renunciation of the Devil.

1. Those who desired to become members of the church, called catechumens, were required to renounce the Devil and all his ways.

2. Heretics were called "weeds of the devil."[21]

3. Renouncing the Devil and performing exorcisms on those who desired to convert from paganism to Christianity were universal in the early church.[22] (This does not mean that all pagans were viewed as demonized, but that all pagans were coming from the world of demonic influences into the body of Christ, dominated by the Holy Spirit.)

---

[19]Secular author Arthur Lyons notes, "Christianity [in the early period] was much too busy fighting for its own survival to search out Satan in any lair in which he might be hiding" (*Satan Wants You*, 23).

[20]Some speculate that demons are a different kind of spiritual creation from fallen angels (who are kept in bondage by God) or that demons are the disembodied spirits of some pre-Adamic race that was destroyed by God during a "gap" creation (between Genesis 1:1 and 1:2); and some refuse to speculate on the origin of demons at all.

[21]Ignatius, quoted by Rev. Francis X. Gokey, *The Terminology for the Devil and Evil Spirits in the Apostolic Fathers* (Washington, D.C.: Catholic University of America Press, 1961), 77.

[22]See, for example, Anne Field, *From Darkness to Light* (Ann Arbor, Mich.: Servant Books, 1978), 71–81.

4. Many churches today still include formal renunciation of the Devil as part of admission to the congregation.[23]

C. *Developed "satanism" apparently did not yet exist.*

   1. Nothing in the writings of the apostolic fathers directly supports any idea that, at the time, other individuals or groups understood the Christian concept of Satan and knowingly worshiped that personage.

   2. Ignatius spoke of anyone who foments disunity in local churches as "serving the devil,"[24] but he meant the same as the teaching that anyone who opposes the one true God is, by default, serving God's enemy.

IV. The Early Middle Ages (A.D. 400–1000)

The church developed a coherent theology over time in response to challenges to faith. The church also developed a coherent demonology, or doctrine concerning Satan and evil, in response to questions and challenges to commonly accepted beliefs.

A. *Contributions from Islamic Demonology*

   1. Elements common to Islam and Christianity fostered common ideas of demonology.

      a. Both adhere to a strict monotheism and a God who is good and sovereign.

      b. Both developed in the Middle East amid common polytheistic religious diversity.

      c. Islam was developing as a religion around the same time Christianity was developing a more comprehensive demonology (seventh century).

   2. Islam and Christianity hold some ideas of demonology in common.

      a. The Muslim terms used to refer to the Devil are *Iblis* and *Shaytan.* Shaytan is not only a pagan Arabic word perhaps related to "to be far from," but was also used by Muhammad in the same way as its linguistically related Hebrew equivalent *Satan* to mean "adversary" or "opponent."[25]

      b. Islam also teaches the fall of Satan through pride and his banishment from heaven by God (Islam's Allah); Satan's temptation of Adam and Eve; and Satan's role as the tempter of humanity.

---

[23]This includes Roman Catholics, Eastern Orthodox, and other sacramental churches such as the Lutheran, Anglican, and Episcopal, as well as most Christian congregations in largely pagan societies.

[24]Gokey, *The Terminology for the Devil*, 70.

[25]Jeffrey Burton Russell, *Lucifer* (Ithaca, N.Y.: Cornell University Press, 1984), 54.

    c. Islam teaches that although God (Allah) is the creator of Satan and other evil spirits, he is not directly responsible for their evil actions (in opposition to dualism).

    d. Many of the evil prankster traits of Islamic *jinn*, or evil spirits, were adopted by Christians during the early Middle Ages as the actions of demons. Jinn, or demons, could hide small objects, trip horses, spoil the day's stew, or perform other relatively small inconveniences and troubles.

    e. Some folklore characteristic of Arabic culture that was adopted into Islam also found its way into Christian demonology, including wings as a symbol of divine or spirit-being power and horns as symbols of power and fertility.

3. The church of the Middle Ages denounced Islam as "devilish" (i.e., pagan).

    a. Muhammad's "evangelism by the sword" resulted in the deaths of thousands of Christians, sparking widespread Christian hatred of Islam and counter-fighting and killing between Christians and Muslims.

    b. Rumors and "myths" about Islam were perpetuated in a church fearful of Islamic persecution.

      (1) Tales were told of horrible desecrations of Jewish and Christian holy sites in Palestine by Muslim conquerors.

      (2) Tales were told of Muslim torture and murder of Christian women and children.

      (3) Tales were told of supernatural Muslim power against Christians derived from their demons, or jinn.

      (4) Tales were told of Islam's fulfillment of biblical prophecy regarding the end of the world and the rise of the antichrist. Some even declared that Muhammad was equivalent to the 666 of the Beast.[26]

B. *Relationship Between Demonology and Folklore/Folk Religions*

1. Definition

    a. Folklore "is the traditional knowledge of the folk. 'Folk' are small groups of people living in isolation who pass along by word of mouth the information and opinions that enable them to live and thrive. This material has no known author or source. It is ancient and covers a plethora of topics from myths and legends, weather and planting lore, songs and games to medicine and language. Above all, it is oral and is known to a relatively small number."[27]

---

[26]Peter Partner, *The Murdered Magicians: The Templars and Their Myth* (Rochester, Vt.: Thorsons, 1987), 34–35.

[27]Horace Beck, "Our Popular Traditions," in *American Folklore and Legend*, ed. Jane Polley (Pleasantville, N.Y.: Reader's Digest Assn., 1978), 7.

b. Folk religion, often called "popular" or "native" religion, usually refers to religious activities and beliefs of a localized social group or culture that lack the complexity or comprehensiveness of a major world religion.

c. For the purposes of this survey, *folklore* will be used in a broad sense to refer to elements of folklore and/or folk religion that influenced Christian ideas about Satan.

2. The spread of Christianity through pagan Europe

a. Christianity was spread throughout Europe by a combination of methods.

(1) Personal evangelism

The evangelism practiced in the New Testament church by the apostle Paul and others spread Christianity on an individual basis as Christians moved into areas of Europe.

(2) Government-sanctioned missionary activities

Christianity was spread on a more organized, large-scale basis through the efforts of missionaries who traveled with military units, explorers, and settlers. These missionaries were commissioned by the church for full-time evangelism.

(3) Mass conversion through military victory

After the eighth century, as the feudal system developed amid frequent fighting between small kingdoms, mass conversion through military victory took place. This was the least effective method of evangelism, being based on brute force, and provided the greatest vulnerability for nominally Christian populations to retain elements of their pagan religions.

b. Christianity's response to paganism was relatively peaceful yet effective.

(1) The early church, considering paganism equivalent to serving Satan, fought against paganism on a spiritual, educational, and philosophical-theological level rather than politically or militarily.

(2) Consequently, paganism declined throughout the Empire gradually over several centuries.

Historian Ronald Hutton notes, "The impression is that all over the Roman world between the mid-fourth and mid-sixth centuries, paganism was in peaceful, gradual and erratic decline.... and it comes to an end imperceptibly in the sixth century when the last of the old religions apparently disappear."[28]

---

[28]Ronald Hutton, *The Pagan Religions of the Ancient British Isles* (Oxford: Blackwell, 1991), 258.

(3) One reason for paganism's decline is that most pagan religions embraced localized polytheism and thus were unable to unite successfully with other small pagan religions against the universal exclusivistic monotheism of Christianity.

(4) A second reason Christianity gradually replaced paganism is that (with few exceptions) most emperors from Constantine (fourth century) on were Christian and thus it was the favored religion of the ruling parties.

(5) Although some contemporary witches and satanists try to portray historic Christianity as unrelentingly murderous against pagans, such is not the case. Until the fifteenth century the church consistently fought paganism with evangelism and education and acted against others who for political or pagan reasons sought to kill pagan worshipers.[29]

3. Folklore additions to assumptions or popular conceptions of Satan[30]

   a. Folklore that came to be associated with Satan usually characterized him as evil but also as ridiculous or a buffoon. This was distinct from the formal church teaching regarding Satan, which focused on philosophical and theological ideas of evil and its implications.

   b. Folklore also contributed ghosts, monsters, wereanimals, dwarves and elves, leprechauns, brownies,[31] mares,[32] trolls, and other magical creatures popularly associated with demons.

   c. Examples of beliefs borrowed from pagan religions

      (1) The Celts' belief in the lord of fertility, Cernunnos, also the god of the underworld (similar to the Greek/Roman Pan) contributed the idea of Satan as horned.

      (2) The folklore of the Germanic people about their gods, such as Thor's red costume and Hilda's sometime appearance as a horrible hag, added to Christian folklore about Satan.

4. Names for Satan originating in folklore

   a. Different folkloric traditions have provided nicknames for Satan, including "Old Horny, Old Hairy, Black Bogey, Lusty Dick, Gentleman Jack, Old Nick, and Old Scratch."[33]

---

[29]Ibid., 256–57. The killing of "infidels" during the Crusades was politically motivated rather than primarily religious in nature.

[30]For a more comprehensive review of this fascinating issue, see Russell's *Lucifer*, chap. 4, "Folklore," 62–91.

[31]A small brown elf or magical creature of Scottish folklore.

[32]From which we get "nightmares."

[33]Russell, *Lucifer*, 66.

b. Folklore names for other magical creatures crept into fairy tales with Christian values, such as Charlot, Heinekin, Rumpelstiltskin, Tom Thumb, and even Robin Hood.[34]

5. Common idioms borrowed from folklore and applied to Satan

   a. Some phrases have come into ordinary speech and are applied without conscious reference to the evil of Satan: "handsome devil," "cute little devil," or "devil-may-care attitude."

   b. Some idioms have a more clear application to Satan, but retain a cavalier sense of him as more annoying than truly threatening evil: "What the Devil!", "What in Devil's name?", "between the Devil and the deep blue sea," "give the Devil his due," and "speak of the Devil."

6. Animal associations borrowed from folklore and applied to Satan

   a. Some associations come from the animals identified with the gods of folk religion. Because from the Christian worldview these gods are false, they are associated with demons.

   b. Other associations come from animals identified with power or from activities folklore attributed to demons.

      (1) Animal associations still prevalent in contemporary western literature (and films) include bats, werewolves, cats, crows/ravens, goats, panthers, spiders, and vultures.

      (2) Some associations relate personal characteristics (e.g., the cat appears vain) and some relate to folk gods (e.g., the raven with Odin, the cat with Hilda, the goat with Pan and Thor).[35]

7. Physical appearances of folklore creatures applied to Satan

   a. Often magical creatures of folklore are physically deformed, such as Rumpelstiltskin's dwarfism, and these attributes were borrowed into Christian folklore concerning Satan:

   "He is lame because of his fall from heaven; his knees are backward; he has an extra face on belly, knees, or buttocks; he is blind; he has horns and a tail; he has no nostrils or only one; he has no eyebrows; his eyes are saucer-like and glow or shoot fire; he has cloven hooves; he emits a sulphurous odor, and when he departs he does so with stench, noise, and smoke; he is covered with coarse, black hair; he has misshapen, batlike wings."[36]

   b. Color symbolism borrowed from folklore includes black as evil, red as symbolic of blood and fire, and sometimes even green, signifying hunting, analogous to some of the pagan gods of the hunt who were later identified by Christians as Satan or at least demonic.

---

[34]The Grimm brothers' collection of Germanic fairy tales contain both the greatest number of clear folklore terminology and superstition and also the clearest principles of Christian metaphors and values.

[35]Russell, *Lucifer*, 67

[36]Ibid., 68.

8. Activities of folklore creatures associated with Satan
   a. Many actions of folklore creatures such as deception, enticement to sin, causing physical or mental illness, and lying are common to what the Bible ascribes to Satan and his demons.
   b. Some actions have been borrowed from folklore and applied to Satan such as stealing children, curdling milk, spoiling eggs, entering through the nose or mouth during sneezing or yawning,[37] and riding animals backward.

9. Folklore pacts adapted to Satan
   a. "Pact" stories (wherein an individual makes an agreement, vow, or "pact" with the Devil) in the Christian tradition date from as early as one recounted by St. Jerome in the fifth century and include the still-popular stories of Mephistopheles, Faust, and "The Devil and Daniel Webster."
   b. Some pact stories are adapted to diabology as a method of frightening hearers into remaining faithful and avoiding evil.
   c. Some pact stories follow their folklore roots closely with the idea that Satan can be tricked or foiled by the clever person who can avoid his pact through his own wit. This theme had the double effect of warning people to avoid evil and affirming that ordinary people with common sense can overcome Satan's wiles.

   Jeffrey Burton Russell presents several popular forms of this kind of pact:
   (1) Satan builds a house for a cobbler who agrees to give him his soul as soon as his candle gutters out, but the cobbler tricks Satan by blowing out the candle before it can burn down.
   (2) A girl agrees to marry Satan as soon as the church service candle burns down, but the quick-thinking priest swallows the lit candle.
   (3) A man wagers his soul in a card game with Satan and agrees to give him his soul when he dies, whether he's buried inside or outside the church; the man then orders that he be buried in the church wall.[38]

   d. Some pact stories became associated with ethnic or religious discrimination against, for example, Jews, gypsies, and Muslims. In these stories, the ethnic group as a whole is supposed to have made a pact with the Devil.

10. Folklore remedies and manipulative magic assumed into Christianity
    a. Charms, healing rituals, and superstitions were not generally con-

---

[37]The origin of our customary "God bless you" after someone sneezes.

[38]Russell, *Lucifer*, 75–76.

sidered satanic by nature, but only satanic if practiced in the name of Satan or a pagan deity.

(1) They were comparable to our contemporary medicine, therapy, insurance, and health food preoccupations.

(2) "Such magic had, in the eyes of its practitioners or purchasers, nothing to do with the great contest between God and Satan: it was concerned with the morally neutral forces of nature, which could be turned to good or bad effect just like the physical natural world."[39]

b. Even during the witch crazes of the later Middle Ages (see Section VI below), most of those prosecuted for practicing "witchcraft" or "diabolism" were convicted not because of their practices *per se*, but because they were accused of practicing them in the name of Satan or pagan deities.

C. *Theological Developments in Early Medieval Demonology*

1. Augustine (A.D. 354–430)

a. Augustine provided the first philosophical foundation for demonology.

b. It was described through his allegory of the "city of God," or "heavenly city," and the "evil city" or "earthly city."

c. His view, which became the prevailing view of the church, is summarized by Russell:

"Two cities exist. One is the heavenly city, whose inhabitants long for God. They view the world as a temporary lodging on the road to their true native land. The other is the earthly city, whose inhabitants scuttle about after the pleasures fetched by greed, lust, envy, and the other sins, deluding themselves that such poor food provides true nourishment. The cosmos was first divided into these two distinct communities when the angels fell; later Adam, and then Cain, inducted humanity into the earthly city. The evil angels and evil humans together occupy that city, while the heavenly city is inhabited by good angels and humans. . . . Fallen angels and fallen humans may recognize that Christ is God, but if they do, their understanding springs not from love but from fear, and they derive no benefit from it. They understand the cosmos only to hate it and its maker."[40]

2. The Council of Braga (A.D. 563)

a. This was not an ecumenical council (i.e., a council representing the entire church), so its effects were limited geographically and ecclesiastically.

---

[39]Hutton, *The Pagan Religions of the Ancient British Isles*, 290.

[40]Jeffrey Burton Russell, *Satan, The Early Christian Tradition* (Ithaca, N.Y.. Cornell University Press, 1981), 216–18.

b. Its strong stand against the Priscillian dualists affirmed that Satan was not a coequal adversary to God, but was a limited, created being subject to God's limiting power.

3. Gregory the Great (pope from A.D. 590 to 604)

a. Gregory reemphasized the biblical demonology of the early church fathers.

b. He officially sanctioned the idea common among clerics of his day that Satan had been an archangel, perhaps the highest angel, before his willful fall and that the depths of his banishment by God was as extremely low as his previous position was high.

c. Gregory attempted to deal with difficult theological tensions.

For example, if Satan (created Lucifer) was created by God, then in what way can God be accountable for Satan's sin and fall without somehow attributing evil or sin to God's nature? Also, if Christ conquered the power of Satan on the cross, why do we still see him and his demons affecting believers and nonbelievers in the same ways and apparently to the same degree as before the cross? How can we affirm the triumph of the cross with the evidence of continuing evil?

4. Isidore (A.D. 560 to 636)

a. Isidore affirmed Gregory's teachings, including his identification of the Antichrist as Satan.[41]

b. He added the idea of ranks or levels of both angels and demons.

c. He broadened the acceptance of the antidualism of the canons (statements) of Braga throughout the church.

5. The ransom versus sacrifice theories of the Atonement

a. The ransom theory (as described by early theologians such as Origen) is that God "ransomed" sinners from Satan—who is called "the god of this world"—by means of Christ's death on the cross. This theory was probably the most popular until Anselm's critique, although no particular view was affirmed as "the" orthodox theory.

b. The sacrifice theory (as described by early medieval theologians such as Haymo and Bede) is that Christ was sacrificed on behalf of sinful humanity to God as just payment for human sin. This theory developed into the satisfaction theory of the later Middle Ages (God's honor and the debt of man's sin were "satisfied" or paid for by Christ's death on the cross).

6. Christ's "Descent into Hell"

---

[41]According to Russell, the identification of the Antichrist with a single individual promoted by Satan as the last judgment approaches was the more ancient view (this antichrist was commonly identified as Nero) and the one to which the Christian church returned in the tenth century. Additionally, "For some writers the Antichrist was the form that Lucifer would take at the world's end when he pitches his last desperate battle against the Lord" (Russell, *Lucifer*, 103).

    a. The meaning of this phrase has been problematic since the first century, when it became associated with the three days Christ's body lay in the tomb.

    b. Various explanations were given to explain this phrase. Some say that "hell" in this instance means "the grave." Others say "hell" means the resting place of the righteous who died before Christ and could not ascend to heaven without Christ (some even taught that Christ preached to the ignorant dead as well and gave them an opportunity to be saved at that point). Another view is that Christ battled with Satan to ransom the dead in "hell."

7. Satanic temptation versus human responsibility (the power of Satan over believers)

    In the earlier Middle Ages, the prevailing view was one of personal moral responsibility, with Satan or his demons providing temptation that could be resisted and overcome quickly and easily by ordinary believers. In the later Middle Ages, this prevailing view was gradually supplanted by the idea that Satan and his demons were so powerful and pervasive that even monks, priests, and nuns were repeatedly and brutally attacked by them and relief took extensive prayer and time.

D. Demonology in Early Medieval Art and Literature

1. The earliest artistic representation of Satan is a mosaic from the sixth century, depicting Satan being judged by Christ.

2. Artistic representations of the Devil did not become common until the ninth century, usually in connection with illustrations of the lives of the saints, whose stories frequently included battles with evil.

3. Art in the early Middle Ages frequently depicted biblical stories involving Satan or other demons.

4. Humanoid demonic figures date from the sixth century and were dominant from the ninth through the eleventh centuries.[42]

5. "Imps," or small, black, misshapen evil creatures, often represent demons in early Middle Ages art.[43]

6. Most figures were asymmetrical or grotesque, symbolizing how fallen, unnatural, and deprived of beauty, truth, and love are demons.

---

[42]Russell, *Lucifer*, 130.

[43]"Because this equation [of depicting pagan gods as demons] was made so frequently, Christians began depicting the Devil in the ways the pagans viewed their gods. . . .The goatee, the cloven feet, the horns, the wrinkled skin, the nakedness and the semi-animal form bear direct reference to both the Greek and Roman god Pan and to the Celtic god Cernunnos, while the female breasts, which appear often in seventeenth-century English depictions of the Devil, came almost certainly from the fertility goddess Diana" (Brian P. Levack, *The Witch-Hunt in Early Modern Europe* [New York: Longman, 1987], 28).

7. The development of "morality," "miracle," and "mystery" plays in the tenth and eleventh centuries incorporated many of the popular characteristics and habits attributed to Satan and his demons.[44]
8. *Beowulf* is the most prominent Old English epic, combining Christian and Teutonic motifs with allusions to the demonic.[45]
9. "The Harrowing of Hell" is an Old English work developed from older Latin works, depicting Christ's alleged battle against Satan in hell during the three days his body lay in the tomb.
10. The Old English poem "Christ and Satan" depicts the fall and condemnation of Satan and his demons, who refuse to accept the world as God has created it and yet who cannot change it.[46]

E. *Summary of Early Middle Ages Demonology*

1. All nonbelievers (pagans) were considered in some way under demonic influence, since all unbelief eventually can be traced to Satan, "the father of lies" (John 8:44).
2. Demonic influence through pagan belief was combatted by education (catechism), preaching of the gospel, and (with the cooperation of the individual) exorcism before convert baptism.
3. Folklore, superstitions, and other kinds of folk medicine were not considered demonic or witchcraft in themselves, but only if they were used in conjunction with heresy or paganism.
4. The arrival of Christianity in some parts of Europe actually halted persecution of some witches.
   "The earliest law codes issued by the northern invaders of the Roman Empire specify penalties for women who were believed to go abroad at night and destroy men by magic. Then these clauses were revoked, often explicitly at the insistence of churchmen. The Lombard code of 643 may serve as an example: 'Let nobody presume to kill a foreign serving maid or female slave as a witch, for it [destruction by magic] is not possible, nor ought to be believed by Christian minds.'"[47]
5. Many of the popular attributes, descriptions, and fables about Satan and demons were incorporated from folk ideas and were used generally to ridicule them. Often they were also mingled with church customs, such as choosing November 1 as All Saints' Day to accommodate folk religion harvest festival customs.[48]

---

[44]Philip Schaff, *History of the Christian Church*, 8 vols. (1890; repr. Grand Rapids: A P & A Publications, n.d.), 5:371–72.

[45]Although the earliest manuscript copy of *Beowulf* is at the end of the early Middle Ages (late tenth or early eleventh century), it was composed much earlier, perhaps as early as the seventh century, certainly by the end of the eighth (Russell, *Lucifer*, 147, fn. 46).

[46]Russell, *Lucifer*, 142.

[47]Hutton, *The Pagan Religions of the Ancient British Isles*, 257.

[48]Schaff, *History of the Christian Church*, 4:206.

6. In terms of the church's formal teaching and practice, the primary focus in demonology was on theological, academic, and biblical issues, not on popular or folk issues.

7. Toward the end of this period, demonology spread to a more popular level with the popular proliferation of "miracle stories" of the saints, who were pictured fighting demonic powers as well as persecution, human evil, and natural calamities.[49]

8. Some Christians in Europe engaged in speculation that the end of the first thousand years would signal the end of the world, including the Battle of Armageddon, the rise of the Beast, the Antichrist and the False Prophet, and the final judgment and condemnation of Satan, all his demons, and all wicked people. While these speculations encouraged some more credulous people to focus on bizarre tales of "signs" and fierce spiritual battles signaling the end, the church never officially promoted, approved, or circulated any of these speculations.[50]

V. The Medieval Scholastic Period (A.D. 1000–1490)[51]

A. Scholasticism Defined

1. "Scholasticism" refers to a certain theological method in which doctrine is explained systematically and philosophically.

2. Scholastic theologians arranged their discussion in a question-answer format, setting forth divergent opinions on a given subject and offering the preferred solution.

3. The scholastics used reason and philosophy along with theology in their resolution of complex theological problems.

B. Scholastic Development of Ideas

1. Scholasticism's focus on reason and critical thinking allowed more complex theological ideas to develop from the earlier arguments based on Scripture and tradition.

2. Because Scripture does not discuss angels or demons at length, some scholastic arguments concerning demonology, while elaborate and comprehensive, were exceptionally speculative.

3. The day-to-day role of Satan and demons in human moral and spiritual affairs was reduced or denigrated into buffoonery.

---

[49]See especially the stories collected by Gregory the Great in his *Dialogues*. Russell notes, "Gregory intended the miracles to summon to our minds the understanding of God's eternal vigilance against the power of evil in a corrupted world" (*Lucifer*, 157). The miracles plays are also discussed in Schaff, *History of the Christian Church*, 5:378.

[50]Yuri Rubinsky and Ian Wiseman, *A History of the End of the World* (New York: Quill Books, 1982), 63.

[51]More regarding demonological developments during this period is available in Schaff, *History of the Christian Church*, 5:375–79.

27

C. *Important contributions to demonology were made during the scholastic period.*

1. Anselm (Archbishop of Canterbury 1093–1109)

   a. His *Fall of the Devil* (1085–1090) "was, in large part a philosophical treatise on the meaning of 'nothing' as applied to evil."[52]

   b. Building on the foundation laid earlier by Augustine, Anselm developed a more complete theory of evil, becoming "the first Christian theologian to confront the nature of evil and other questions with a logically systematic rational process."[53]

   c. Like Augustine, he defined evil as privation in two different senses:

      (1) A lack of divine perfection in created beings

      (2) A lack in something of an attribute it should possess (blindness in an eagle, immorality in a man, etc.)

   d. He wrestled with the problem of predestination and free will, seeking to answer how God could be sovereign and yet not the direct cause of Satan's (or man's) fall into evil.

      (1) Anselm argued that God sovereignly determines all conditions, including the condition that angels and humans have the capacity for truly free moral choices.

      (2) He also argued that for angelic or human choices to be truly free, the choices themselves cannot be conditioned, only the capacity for the choices.

      (3) Therefore God remains sovereign, but Lucifer and Adam are morally and spiritually responsible for their sinning and God is not the cause (or conditioner) of evil.

   e. Anselm argued that Satan and his demons can operate only in a limited way with God's permission and that Satan has no proprietary rights over mankind at all.

   f. Anselm taught that Satan and his temptations were unnecessary to cause Adam's fall or the sinful actions of any subsequent human beings. That is, Adam was entirely capable of committing sin apart from outside influences.

2. Peter of Lombard (1100–1160)

   a. Peter collected and systematized varying positions on theological issues, presenting the best arguments for and against divergent views, including views of demonology.

   b. Peter preserved some more speculative arguments of previous theologians, such as the nature of angelic "bodies."

   c. "Peter Lombard noted that Lucifer and the other angels were created with natural goodness (*boni*); they were neither naturally evil

---

[52]Russell, *Lucifer*, 162.

[53]Ibid.

(*mali*) nor damned (*miseri*). Yet since they were also not confirmed in goodness (*beati*), they were prone to sin."[54]

    d. Peter agreed with Anselm that Satan had no *rights* over humanity, but he attributed greater powers of temptation and evil to Satan than did Anselm.

  3. Catharians (1140s through the end of the Middle Ages)

    a. Cathar dualism, declared as heresy in the church, elevated the power of Satan and focused on what the Cathars viewed as the never-ending, never-winnable battle between good and evil.

    b. This focus on epic battles of spiritual powers popularized ideas about Satan and demons in art, literature, drama, and popular sermons.

    c. Cathar dualists borrowed from earlier dualists, many of whom emphasized mystical experiences of spiritual battles.

    d. Cathar dualists taught that the material world was created and dominated by Satan, that the God of the Old Testament was actually Satan, that Christ did not have a material body, and that salvation is achieved by recognizing that our bodies are evil and that we can escape them at death and return to spiritual reality with God.[55]

  4. Thomas Aquinas (1225–1274)

    a. Aquinas viewed hell as "a state of deprivation of God's presence rather than as a place."[56]

    b. He believed that it was possible for demons to take on temporary forms to entice men and women to sexual lust (*incubus* and *succubus*).[57]

    c. Aquinas believed that demons could cause people to fly through the air (or at least believe they were flying through the air).[58]

  5. Pope Gregory IX was the first pope officially to associate witchcraft with heresy as an ecclesiastical crime (1233).[59]

D. The scholastic teachings regarding Satan may be summarized as follows:

  1. God permits Satan to tempt believers without violating free-will choices between good and evil.[60]

---

[54]Ibid., 174.

[55]Levack, *The Witch-Hunt in Early Modern Europe*, 38.

[56]Russell, *Lucifer*, 180.

[57]Schaff, *History of the Christian Church*, 5:378–79. See the discussion in point E below.

[58]Ibid.

[59]Ibid., 379.

[60]Levack, *The Witch-Hunt in Early Modern Europe*, 31–32.

2. Satan cannot control men's souls, but he and his demons are sometimes permitted by God to control natural, physical forces, but not by violating natural law.[61]

    a. Demonic wonders use illusion to appear to violate natural law.

    b. Demonic wonders sometimes manipulate natural forces in ways more sophisticated, but not qualitatively different than can man.

3. God created Satan and his demons with good natures, but they violated God's standards by their own free will.

4. Evil is not a substance, person, force, or idea, but is instead an active violation of God's law.

E. *Political, Social, and Religious Developments Leading to the Witch Craze*

1. Incubi and Succubi

    a. One development in demonology in the later Middle Ages that resulted eventually in the witch craze was the idea of demons' having sexual relations with humans.

    b. *Incubi* and *succubi* were said to be demons taking on male or female forms to entice humans, including witches, to have sexual intercourse with them.

    c. The historical source for this belief is uncertain.

        (1) This belief probably did not come from folk religion, although many ancient religious myths speak of sexual intercourse between the "gods" and mankind.

        (2) The distinctive belief concerning demons and humans probably came from folk applications of scholastic demonology, which declared that demons, though sexless and formless, can take on physical forms and perennially seek to entice people into sin, of which sexual sin is a chief evidence.[62]

2. The Crusades

    a. The original goal of the Crusades was to "free" the Holy Land, especially Jerusalem, from Muslim rule.

    b. The Crusades exposed Europeans to magical arts, folk religions, and folk traditions.

    c. Muslim foes provided an easy target for charges of demonism by European Christians because of their religion and their persecution of Christians in lands they dominated.

    d. As more portions of the Middle East came under Muslim control, the Crusades' goals were less far-reaching and "crusade" eventually came to mean any military campaign with a noble, spiritual goal.

---

[61]Ibid., 31.

[62]Russell, *Lucifer*, 183.

e. The Knights Templar was an order of soldier-monks who partici-
pated in the Crusades during the thirteenth century and disbanded
by 1312.

(1) Legends

The legends that came to be associated with the Knights Templar incorporated many of the myths later associated with the
witches of the Great Witch Hunts. Although the Knights were
disbanded in 1312, rumors of continuing secret groups of
Knights have circulated ever since. Aleister Crowley made
himself "Master of a Templar Order" as a symbol of his mastery
of magic.[63] (See Section VII.B.)

(2) Accusations of witchcraft

Because of the unusual customs, stories, and artifacts they
brought back to Europe from Syria during the late thirteenth
century, they were prime candidates to be accused of witchcraft. They were from a strange land and of a unique religious
order, and so little was known about them that they became
scapegoats and object lessons for suspicious people. As the stories about them circulated, new myths and mysteries were
added until every sort of evil or mysterious power or secret
conceivable was somehow associated with them.[64]

VI. The Great Witch Hunts (1490s to 1840s)

A. The Origin of Witchcraft and Satanism Myths

1. Satanism and witchcraft are to be carefully distinguished both historically and in their contemporary manifestations (see Part III, Section I.A). However, misunderstandings of history, theology, and
occultism obscure these distinctions.

2. During this period of church history, the terms for witchcraft and satanism were used interchangeably.

3. During the witch hunts of this period, many folk practices and beliefs
were confused with this witchcraft.

4. Also during the witch hunts, many stories were made up both by ac-
cusers and by confessed "witches," further confusing any reliable traditions of folk belief, witchcraft, heresy, or occult involvement
(including satanism).

5. During the modern period, inaccurate historical research both by
Christians and by non-Christians has incorrectly identified and mis-

---

[63] Partner, *Murdered Magicians* xx,

[64] See Partner's carefully researched book for accurate information on the Templars and the Templar
legends.

attributed characteristics, practices, and beliefs to "witches," "satanists," and "heretics."

6. Many people (including Christians, non-Christians, and occult practitioners—both witches and satanists) assume the authenticity of these erroneous stories and apply them in some way to contemporary satanism.

7. It is on this basis that we explore the often contradictory and complex demonology developing throughout this period, even though we recognize that there is no unbroken historical connection between this demonology and contemporary satanism.

B. *The Reformation and Post-Reformation Influences on the Witch Hunts*

1. The early Reformation period saw the most intense witch-hunting, the greatest numbers of prosecutions, and the highest rates of conviction and execution.[65]

2. This increase in activity was due in part to the widespread religious conflict between Catholic and Protestant communities.

   Brian P. Levack records, "In the most general terms it made communities more fearful of religious and moral subversion, more aware of the presence of Satan in the world, and more eager therefore to rid their communities of corrupting, subversive influences, the most obvious and vulnerable of whom were witches."[66]

3. However, "if witch-hunting was more widespread and intense in areas that were religiously divided, then the converse was also true. Religiously homogenous or monolithic states generally experienced only occasional witch-hunts and relatively low numbers of executions."[67]

4. The coming of the Enlightenment did not end the witch hunts, which actually were worse from 1550 to 1650 than at any other time.

   H. R. Trevor-Roper explains that "there can be no doubt that the witch-craze grew, and grew terribly, after the Renaissance. Credulity in high places increased, its engines of expression were made more terrible, more victims were sacrificed to it.... Nor was the craze entirely separable from the intellectual and spiritual life of those years. It was forwarded by the cultivated popes of the Renaissance, by the great Protestant reformers, by the saints of the Counter-Reformation, by the scholars, lawyers and churchmen of the age of Scaliger and Lipsius, Bacon and Grotius, Bérulle and Pascal. If those two centuries were an age of light, we have to admit that, in one respect at least, the Dark Age was more civilized.... [and] did its best to disperse these

---

[65]Levack, *The Witch-Hunt in Early Modern Europe*, 95.

[66]Ibid., 109.

[67]Ibid., 106.

relics of paganism which the church of the Middle Ages would afterwards exploit."[68]

5. Only isolated prosecutions and convictions occurred during the eighteenth and nineteenth centuries. Levack attributes this decline partly to the Protestant emphasis on the sovereignty of God, which "led a number of Protestant writers and preachers to deny the Devil's ability to produce certain types of marvels, such as hail storms, and this fostered a scepticism towards *maleficia*, and that in turn developed into a more general scepticism regarding all aspects of witchcraft."[69]

C. *The Difficulty in Verifying Statistics*

1. Statistics are difficult to verify and range widely, depending on the source and how the "witches" are counted.

2. This is an important issue, since false, inflated figures are repeatedly used both by some neo-pagans, to confirm their charge that Christianity launched massive persecutions against them, and by some Christians, to confirm their belief in a widespread satanic conspiracy.[70]

3. Levack explains the difficulty in obtaining accurate statistics:

"Because so many judicial records have been destroyed or otherwise lost, and because the trials of so many witches were never even officially recorded, the total number of witchcraft prosecutions and executions cannot be determined with any degree of accuracy. Some estimates, ranging as high as nine million executions, have been grossly exaggerated. The totals have been inflated both by the claims of witch-hunters themselves, who often boasted about how many witches they had burned, and by subsequent writers, who for different reasons wished to emphasize the gravity of the process they were discussing. Detailed scholarly studies have generally led to a downward estimate of the total numbers of victims. It has long been believed, for example, that an early seventeenth-century witch-hunt in the Basque-speaking Pays de Labourd in France resulted in 600 executions, but it now appears that the actual figure was closer to 80. In Bamberg, where another 600 witches were allegedly burned between 1624 and 1631, the totals are probably closer to 300. And in Scotland, where Henry C. Lea claimed that 7,500 persons were executed for witchcraft, the actual tally is probably less than 1,500."[71]

4. Levack concludes, "Even if we make allowances for trial records that have been lost or destroyed, the total number of persons who were actually tried for witchcraft throughout Europe probably did not

[68]Trevor-Roper, H. R., *The European Witch-Craze of the Sixteenth and Seventeenth Centuries and Other Essays* (New York: Harper & Row, 1967), 91.

[69]Levack, *The Witch-Hunt in Early Modern Europe*, 111.

[70]Edward Geoffrey Parrinder, *Witchcraft: European and African* (New York: Barnes & Noble, 1963), 35.

[71]Levack, *The Witch-Hunt in Early Modern Europe*, 19.

exceed 100,000. . . . It would not be unreasonable to conclude, therefore, that European communities executed about 60,000 witches during the early modern period."[72]

D. The Prosecutions

1. The prosecutions were not a single historical event.

   Levack notes, "The European witch-hunt was not a single historical event or episode but a composite of thousands of individual prosecutions that took place from Scotland to Transylvania and from Spain to Finland over a 300-year period. Although these prosecutions shared many common characteristics, they also arose in different historical circumstances and they often reflected witch-beliefs that were peculiar to a certain locality."[73]

2. Torture was used to secure confessions.

   a. Torture to produce confession was a technique used in many parts of Europe since the Roman times.[74] However, its use changed as a result of the witch hunts.

   b. During the Christian era, torture was used by civil courts primarily to obtain information from prisoners of war and captured spies.

   c. Ecclesiastical courts associated torture with individuals convicted of heresy in order to obtain a confession resulting in reconciliation with the church.

   d. Levack explains that torture was a part of the judicial system before the witch hunts:

   "In their original and strictest form they contained, first of all, a prohibition against the use of torture unless the judge could prove that a crime had in fact been committed. Once that was ascertained, the judge still could not sentence a suspect to be tortured unless there was a solid presumption of guilt (half the proof needed for conviction) or circumstantial evidence (*indicia*) that was the legal equivalent of the testimony of one eye-witness. . . . For both humanitarian and legal reasons rules were also established to restrict the severity and duration of the torture."[75]

   e. As the witch hunts increased in number and intensity, torture began to be used less discriminately and as a tool to produce conviction, rather than a tool for use *after* conviction.

---

[72]Ibid., 19–21.

[73]Ibid., ix.

[74]Trevor-Roper, *The European Witch-Craze*, 118.

[75]Levack, *The Witch-Hunt in Early Modern Europe*, 72–73.

"As it turned out, however, these rules were greatly relaxed and the system was grossly abused. . . . The most significant modification of the rules dealt with the requirement that the judge first establish that a crime had in fact been committed. As John Langbein has argued, if this rule had been strictly enforced, the European witch craze would never have claimed its countless victims."[76]

3. The tortures, confessions, and trials promulgated superstition, ignored rational inquiry and evidentially based defenses, and developed trial systems that convicted the innocent.[77]

4. The worst prosecutions and prosecutors were in Germany, Scotland, France, and Salem, Massachusetts.

   a. In Scotland between 1563 and 1727, 618 persons were tried for witchcraft, of which 216 were executed. The Scots witch hunts were closely tied to the conflicts between the Protestant English rulers and the Catholic Scots nationalists.[78]

   b. In Germany, France, and Eastern Europe the witch hunts proliferated in the largest numbers, over the longest periods of time, and with the highest execution rates. Levack and others suggest reasons for these high rates:

      (1) The areas involved many small jurisdictions that operated free from most centralized temperance and control.

      (2) The areas were in the midst of the strongest Reformation conflicts, not only between Protestants and Catholics, but among the Protestant groups as well.

      (3) Heinrich Institoris and Jacob Sprenger, authors of the infamous witch hunt manual, the *Malleus Maleficarum* (see point E below), traveled throughout these areas spearheading the local witch hunts and "training" inquisitors to work after they left.

      (4) The devastation of the Black Plague was greatest here and people were more likely to believe in the destructive powers of dark and evil forces.[79]

5. The pockets of temperance were in Spain, England, and Italy.

   a. Some clerics spoke out against the witch hunts, such as the Dutch priest Cornelius Loos Callidus, who was imprisoned for declaring that confessions made under torture might not be true (1593); and Dr. Dietrich Flade, who was burned at the stake for speaking against the prosecution of witchcraft (1589).[80]

---

[76]Ibid., 73–74.

[77]Schaff, *History of the Christian Church*, 6:238.

[78]Levack, *The Witch-Hunt in Early Modern Europe*, 20.

[79]See Levack, Parrinder, and Trevor-Roper.

[80]Schaff, *History of the Christian Church*, 6:241.

b. During the Spanish Inquisition against the Jews and the Jewish *Conversos* to Christianity, the inquisitors actually restrained persecution of supposed witches.[81] In fact, the "Inquisition in Spain checked the popular and civil efforts to destroy witches and it protected their lives. Its efforts were notably successful in 1611 when the inquisitor Salazar Frias examined 1,800 cases, compiled masses of evidence, and submitted his report to the Suprema. He gave many instances to show that witches were the subjects of delusions and that many confessions had been extracted under torture. Salazar concluded, 'I have not found even indications from which to infer that a single act of witchcraft has really occurred.'"[82]

c. Reason and caution also came from England, where William Harvey, physician to King Charles, investigated allegations of witchcraft and could find none that were not falsely made or fraudulent (1685).[83] English historian Arthur Wilson attended some of the witch trials in Chelmsford and concluded that all the women were deluded, their "fancies working by gross fumes and vapours might make the imagination ready to take any impression."[84]

d. Other contemporary critics are discussed in Trevor-Roper's account of the sixteenth- and seventeenth-century witch hunts.[85]

E. **The Unifying Evil of the Malleus Maleficarum (The Witches' Hammer)**

1. Although there were several small, locally known church manuals for dealing with witchcraft,[86] the work of two agents of Pope Innocent VIII provided Europe with its first textbook for exposing and prosecuting witchcraft.

2. Pope Innocent VIII issued a papal bull against witchcraft in 1484, authorizing Heinrich Institoris and Jacob Sprenger to investigate and prosecute charges of witchcraft throughout the lands under his ecclesiastical control.

3. In 1486, Sprenger and Institoris published *Malleus Maleficarum*, a textbook on witchcraft.

4. This book became the "Bible" of the Great Witch Hunt of the late Middle Ages.[87]

a. It was the single most influential factor in promulgating false information about satanism, witchcraft, folklore, and folk medicine

---

[81]Levack, *The Witch-Hunt in Early Modern Europe*, 84.

[82]Parrinder, *Witchcraft: European and African*, 26.

[83]Ibid., 96–97.

[84]Ibid., 98.

[85]Trevor-Roper, *The European Witch-Craze*, 128–34.

[86]Schaff, *History of the Christian Church*, 6:236.

[87]Trevor-Roper, *The European Witch-Craze*, 101–4.

and in providing a pseudo-documentary basis for civil and ecclesiastical courts.[88]

    b. Geoffrey Parrinder declares, "Sprenger, who was the principal author, was a dangerous and evil-minded fanatic. He claimed to have gathered disinterested information from eye-witnesses, confessions of witches maintained even to the stake. He revels in the preposterous and even more in the sensual. Altogether the *Malleus* is one of the wickedest and most obscene books ever written."[89]

5. Among the dangerous principles promoted in the book were (1) public rumor is sufficient for an indictment; (2) one who testifies on behalf of a defendant must be bewitched; (3) torture is the quickest way to get a confession and thereby a conviction.[90]

6. Its popularity led to the "general assumption that most fifteenth-century witch-hunting activities occurred under the auspices of papal inquisitors. This is clearly not the case."[91] In actuality, the vast majority of the activities were under civil control and direction.

7. This book, which is still in print, is still used by satanic conspiracy theory advocates as "evidence"; some self-styled satanists and witches use it as a resource for beliefs and practices.

F. The Spanish Inquisition (Fifteenth–Eighteenth Centuries)

1. The Spanish Inquisition was primarily against the Jews of Spain, not against supposed witches. It was commissioned by Pope Sixtus IV (1478), but it was under the supervision of the Spanish crown, and the prosecutors were accountable to the king, not the pope.[92]

2. It was responsible for the reprehensible executions of thousands of Jews,[93] and those who were executed primarily for witchcraft were few. The last victim of the Spanish Inquisition was executed in 1826.[94]

G. Margaret Murray's Confusion of Witch-Hunt Witchcraft with Ancient Paganism

1. Margaret Alice Murray's ground-breaking work in Egyptology produced more than eighty books and articles at the turn of the century.

2. About 1910 she turned her attention to the Great Witch Hunts of Western Europe. Her thesis was that the witches represented a pre-Christian Western European pagan religion that was (in some important ways) superior to Christianity.

---

[88]Schaff, *History of the Christian Church*, 6:237–38.

[89]Parrinder, *Witchcraft: European and African*, 25.

[90]Schaff, *History of the Christian Church*, 6:238.

[91]Levack, *The Witch-Hunt in Early Modern Europe*, 79.

[92]Schaff, *History of the Christian Church*, 6:243–44.

[93]Schaff estimates a total of 195,937 were punished by the Inquisition between 1480 and 1524, and 14,344 were executed (*History of the Christian Church*, 6:251).

[94]Ibid.

3. Murray's *Witch Cult in Western Europe* (1921) was the first attempt to study the witch hunts from a scholarly and historical perspective.
   a. She used only a few published sources and ignored all of the much greater quantity of unpublished sources and records.
   b. She "began with the premise that the trials were of a genuine religion, and reconstructed it from the confessions of the accused and the writings of their prosecutors.... Her treatment of her sources was the utter reverse of impartial. She ignored or misquoted evidence which indicated that the actions attributed to the alleged witches were physically impossible. Or she rationalized it."[95]
   c. "Furthermore, she pruned and rearranged her evidence ruthlessly to support her assertion that the religion concerned was standard throughout Europe."[96]
4. Murray never modified or abandoned her theories regardless of criticism, contrary evidence, or her own further study. She contributed the section on witchcraft to the *Encyclopaedia Britannica* editions between 1929 and 1968, which undeservedly popularized her theory and gave it authority among the general public. Her books, *The God of the Witches* (1933) and *The Divine King of England* (1954) repeated her errors.
5. Among the errors fostered by Murray:
   a. Those who confessed were truly witches and not innocent people tortured into confessing.
   b. Witches' covens were limited to thirteen members—even though almost everyone was tried individually.
   c. Witches' holidays were four and corresponded to the seasonal quarters—although the "confessions" scattered holidays throughout the year.
   d. The terms *Sabbath* and *esbat* described the witches' rituals and "business" meetings, whereas it was actually the prosecutors who chose the term *Sabbath* as a mockery to Judaism, and the term *esbat* occurs only in one minor French source.
   e. The witches' ceremonies were of ancient pagan origin, when in actuality they are a clear parody of contemporary Christian ceremonies and morals.
   f. Satan is identified with any horned deity in any religion throughout Europe, the Middle East, and Rome and Greece, even though the deities of the various ethnic groupings had divergent origins.
   g. This "Old Religion" was of universal scope, even though only a minuscule number of males were ever prosecuted or convicted.[97]

---

[95]Hutton, *The Pagan Religions of the Ancient British Isles,* 302.

[96]Ibid., 302–3.

[97]See ibid., 302–6.

VII. Satanism in the Modern Period

A. *The Anti-Religion of the Enlightenment as Foundational to Modern Satanism*

1. Anti-morality is foundational to contemporary satanism and can be found among various groups in history.

   a. The Reformation did not provide the only option for those disaffected from the Roman Catholic church. The freedom of thought that supported the Reformation also allowed for the freedom to reject Christianity and supernaturalism, which many intellectuals and aristocrats in Europe did beginning in the sixteenth century.

   b. For many religion simply became unimportant.

   c. For others, religion was an evil to be rejected and scorned.

2. Some of those who rejected and scorned Christianity formed secular associations (both formal and informal) where they not only celebrated their human autonomy from God, but also mocked the church, its beliefs, and its practices.

   a. The earliest social literary ridicule of the Roman church came from a sixteenth-century French former priest and monk, François Rabelais (1494–1553), who rejected Roman Catholicism and Calvinism and instead embraced a stoic philosophy that defined the Christian life as education, self-discipline, and self-reliance. Although he did not reject faith altogether, his autonomous ideal community developed in his novel *Gargantua* provided the idea of a community without laws for later groups that rejected all religion.

   b. "Do What You Will" is one of the most popular phrases borrowed both by satanist and by witch and is often erroneously attributed to Aleister Crowley.[98] It actually originated with Rabelais in 1535 as the motto for his imaginary community of sensual delight, Thélème.[99]

   c. Rabelais threw off religious convention in his quest for earthly pleasures. Thélème was the counter-mirror of St. Augustine's City of God and of the monasteries and convents of Rabelais's day.

   d. Rabelais describes life in his imaginary community:

   "All their life was regulated not by laws, statutes, or rules, but according to their free will and pleasure. They rose from bed when they pleased, and drank, ate, worked, and slept when the fancy seized them. Nobody worked them; nobody compelled them either

---

[98]Aleister Crowley's motto is an expanded version; "Do what thou Wilt shall be the whole of the Law; Love is the Law, Love under Will."

[99]The French word *thélème* comes from the Greek word for "will."

to eat or to drink, or to do anything else whatever.... In their rules was only one clause: DO WHAT YOU WILL."[100]

   e. Thélème's escape from law did not include deliberate devil worship or satanic ritual. It did, however, parody the Roman Catholic church and make fun of the Catholic insistence on obedience and devotion to the church and its leaders.

3. Rabelais's anti-religious community set the stage for later anti-morality developments.

   a. The Monks of Medmenham was a seventeenth-century association of European aristocrats who met for gambling, feasting, drinking, and sexual games with courtesans.

   b. The Hell-Fire Clubs of the eighteenth and nineteenth centuries in England were patterned after Thélème and the Monks and included sometimes elaborate mock rituals, including a "Black Mass" that culminated in a raucous drinking and sex party.

   c. Other elitist pleasure clubs included those of aristocrats such as Edmund Curll, Sir Francis Dashwood, and John Montague, the Earl of Sandwich.

   d. These clubs were open only to select aristocrats who had emerged from religious ignorance to embrace the atheistic humanism of the Enlightenment, "in other words, spitting in the eye of the church and the official morality it stood for."[101]

4. The anti-religion of the Enlightenment provided the secular philosophy and rejection of Christianity that is foundational to contemporary satanism.[102]

B. Aleister Crowley (1875–1947)[103]

1. This self-styled occultist, magician, drug addict, and sexual deviant developed a fanatical and often incoherent system of occult magical belief that has been used by more self-styled occultists in this century than any other system.

2. Crowley was raised as a strict, fundamentalist Brethren in England and was the son of a wealthy ale brewer. He was well-educated, but rejected his parents' faith as a young man. At one point his mother called him "the Great Beast" (666) of Revelation, and he later took this title for himself, mocking his mother's faith.

---

[100]Quoted from Rabelais by Geoffrey Ashe, *Do What You Will: A History of Anti-Morality* (New York: W. H. Allen, 1974), 20.

[101]Ibid., 48.

[102]For further information on the history of satanism, see Ashe, *Do What You Will*, and Lyons, *Satan Wants You*, 16–83.

[103]An interesting biography of Crowley is in Leslie Shepart, ed., *Encyclopedia of Occultism and Parapsychology* (Detroit: Gale Research, 1984), 1:282–83.

3. He quickly developed an interest in magic and occultism and joined an occult group called the Hermetic Order of the Golden Dawn in 1898.

4. His continuing quarrels with Golden Dawn leader Samuel Liddell Mathers caused his expulsion, so Crowley formed his own occult society and named it the Order of the Silver Star.

5. Crowley was an accomplished world traveler and writer who used his unusual travels as backdrops for his outrageous prose and poetry, much of which extolled his own sexual exploits, including group sex, bestiality, homosexuality, and drug-enhanced or ritual sex.

6. In *Liber Legis* (The Book of the Law) Crowley announced a new magical era of human history ruled by the "Law of Thélème"—"Do what you will shall be the whole of the Law"—although he removed Rabelais's law from its context of self-discipline and knowledge and placed it in a context of antinomian (i.e., lawless) self-indulgence.

7. Crowley claimed that through natural and drug-induced trance states and through magical sex rituals he encountered demons and other kinds of evil spirits, sometimes even having sex with them.

8. The focus of Crowley's magical system was the individual and one's self-fulfillment and self-indulgence as the highest goal of existence. It combined the three elements of (1) rejection of Christianity, (2) assumption of the supremacy of the self, and (3) the use of magic to enhance one's experiences and reach one's goals. This philosophy became fundamental to contemporary satanism.

C. Gerald Gardner

1. An Englishman, Gardner developed a system of witchcraft (not properly satanism) based on Murray's *Witch Cult in Western Europe*. Much of his symbology, terminology, and ceremonial instructions were borrowed from Murray and provided ritual patterns for self-styled satanists today, even though they reject his witchcraft system.

2. Gardner claims to be descended from a long line of "Old Religion wise ones" and to have inherited the secrets of the religion and its magic.

3. He claimed that he was unable to reveal his witchcraft until England (in 1951) repealed its "repressive" Witchcraft Act of 1736.

   a. He fostered a false interpretation of the law that is still accepted today.

   b. Actually, "This [statute] was not the survivor of the murderous statutes of the early modern period, but their very antithesis.... Its fundamental principle was that witchcraft and magic did not exist, and that belief in them was part of a childish and more barbaric age. It therefore forbade anybody to accuse another person of practising either, and prescribed a maximum of a year's imprisonment for anyone who *claimed* to practise either. Henceforth people were in no danger of being hauled into court because their enemies suspected them of witchcraft, and in theory nobody could suffer for engaging in it in private. But any self-styled witch, magician or fortune-teller who advertised her or his craft was vulnerable to prosecution."[104]

4. Gardner's system borrows ideas, types, ceremonies, incantations, and images from many different religious and magical systems, including Crowley's Ordo Templi Orientis. It is notoriously historically inaccurate, and relies to a great extent on Murray's works.

5. Gardner's is still the most widely known of the contemporary witchcraft systems and is the source of such activities as "the bound and blindfolded initiation; the symbolic scourging; the ceremonial focus of a circle containing an altar; the use of pentagrams and triangles; the invocation and banishment of spirits; the appeal to the guardians of the four cardinal points of the compass; the use of incense and water; the notion that divine forces are drawn into one or more of the celebrants; and the impedimenta[105] of a sword and two knives, one black- and one white-handled."[106]

6. Gardner's is a witchcraft system, not a satanic system, although some self-styled satanists borrow from his works.

7. Some people use his system to "validate" their claims to have descended from a long line of magical practitioners.

8. Some satanic conspiracy advocates use the same kind of argument to lend credence to the unsupported idea that there are unbroken generations of satanists conspiring to destroy the church.

D. Anton Szandor LaVey: The High Priest of the Church of Satan

1. Biographical data

   a. LaVey was born April 11, 1930.

   b. He was divorced from Carole, his first wife. Their daughter, Karla, actively promoted her father's Church of Satan.

   c. He had a long common-law marriage to a woman named Diane. Their daughter, Zeena, became the Church of Satan spokesperson.

   d. With his current companion, Blanche Barton, who is also his biographer, he has a young son, Satan Xerxes Carnacki LaVey.

2. The development of a nontheology

   a. LaVey's teenage years as a traveling carnival worker and organ player gave him a cynicism toward Christianity and a skepticism toward altruism.

   Biographer Burton Wolfe quoted LaVey, "On Saturday night I would see men lusting after half-naked girls dancing at the carnival, and on Sunday morning when I was playing organ for the tent-

---

[104]Hutton, *The Pagan Religions of the Ancient British Isles*, 331.

[105]"Impedimenta" in this context refers to the ritual tools used by the witch.

[106]Hutton, *The Pagan Religions of the Ancient British Isles*, 333.

show evangelists at the other end of the carnival lot, I would see these same men sitting in the pews with their wives and children, asking God to forgive them and purge them of carnal desires. And the next Saturday night they'd be back at the carnival or some other place of indulgence. I knew then that the Christian church thrives on hypocrisy, and that man's carnal nature will out no matter how much it is purged or scourged by any white-light religion."[107]

b. LaVey's brief involvement during his late teens with militant Israeli groups and other groups deemed "subversive" by the FBI led him to compare that kind of government suspicion as "not far removed from the church-induced hysteria which had caused thousands to be burned at the stake as witches and sorcerers, simply because they threatened the wrong people."[108]

c. His first visit to an organized group of "devil worshipers" was to a chapter of the Order of Thélèma, followers of Aleister Crowley, but he was disappointed with their "bland" ideas and practices.[109]

3. The development of a church

a. LaVey states, "The church of Satan *evolved* from a group of like-minded individuals."[110]

b. Throughout the 1950s, LaVey and his first wife, Carole, entertained in their home. Their guests were fellow nonconformists, literary dilettantes, and humanists who enjoyed LaVey's often impromptu magic acts, lectures, and other kinds of provocative performances. LaVey called these informal meetings his "Magic Circle."[111]

c. By the early 1960s, LaVey formalized his magic lectures and added lectures and demonstrations on a variety of occult subjects. His lecture on the Black Mass concluded with a ritual developed by LaVey himself. LaVey called the Black Mass "the original psychodrama—purging the participants of the pain induced by certain societal sacred cows through a lavish ritual of ridicule, parody and satire."[112]

d. LaVey envisioned his church as a recruiting ground for an exclusive, loosely knit group of enlightened individuals who would throw off the chains of convention, base social conformity, religious oppression, and animal stupidity and embrace "the only

---

[107]Anton Szandor LaVey, *The Satanic Bible* (New York: Avon Books, 1969), introduction by Burton H. Wolfe, 12.

[108]Barton, *The Secret Life of a Satanist*, 56.

[109]Ibid., 61.

[110]Interview, 5 August 1994.

[111]Barton, *The Secret Life of a Satanist*, 74ff.

[112]Ibid., 77.

counterculture, rational alternative,"[113] the freedom of fully realized human potential.[114]

4. The Satanic "creed"

The "creed" of the Church of Satan is "The Nine Satanic Statements," widely published by that Church and composed by Anton LaVey.

a. Satan represents indulgence instead of abstinence.

b. Satan represents vital existence instead of spiritual pipe dreams.

c. Satan represents undefiled wisdom instead of hypocritical self-deceit.

d. Satan represents kindness to those who deserve it instead of love wasted on ingrates.

e. Satan represents vengeance instead of turning the other cheek.

f. Satan represents responsibility to the responsible instead of concern for psychic vampires.

g. Satan represents man as just another animal—sometimes better, more often worse than those that walk on all fours—who, because of his "divine spiritual and intellectual development," has become the most vicious animal of all.

h. Satan represents all the so-called sins, as they all lead to physical, mental, or emotional gratification.

i. Satan has been the best friend the church has ever had, as he has kept it in business all these years.[115]

[113]Interview, 5 August 1994.

[114]Barton, *The Secret Life of a Satanist*, 119 and also 126, where LaVey is quoted, "I wanted to create a forum, a loosely-structured cabal for the productive aliens, not misfits who need to depend on a group. After the re-organization, I was free to be more selective.... Groups encourage dependence on beliefs and delusions to reinforce their omnipotence rather than applying magic on an individual basis, as *The Satanic Bible* outlines."

[115]LaVey, *The Satanic Bible*, 25.

Part III: Misconceptions About Satanism

I. Beliefs Frequently Confused with Satanism

A. Witchcraft[116]

1. Witchcraft can refer to a contemporary pantheistic movement.

   a. Margot Adler's definitive survey, *Drawing Down the Moon*, recognizes the common contemporary witchcraft beliefs of the divinity of all (pantheism), dualism or pluralism (including polytheism, belief in many deities), and relative morals.[117]

   b. Contemporary witchcraft groups may be of many different traditions, often named after the god or goddess in focus (e.g., Diana). The most popular and public group is Raymond Buckland's Wicca.

   c. Most contemporary witchcraft groups are matriarchal and emphasize the feminine aspect of reality.

      (1) Many contemporary witches assume that the pre-Christian or pre-Judeo-Christian religions and social orders were matriarchal rather than patriarchal.

      (2) This view was first articulated by Johann Jakob Bachofen in 1861 and popularized in the 1960s and later through the books of Elizabeth Gould David, Helen Diner, Robert Graves, Phyllis Chester, and Evelyn Read.

      (3) There is no substantiation for this view, and it is contradicted by the historical evidence.

      Assyriologist-Sumerologist Tikva Frymer-Kensky notes, "The modern literature on the Goddess was alien to my understanding of the worship of these ancient deities. There was not one Goddess, there were many goddesses; they were not enshrined in a religion of women, but in the official religion of male-dominated societies; they were not evidence of ancient mother-worship, but served as an integral part of a religious

---

[116]For a thorough treatment of witchcraft see the volume in this series on that subject by Craig Hawkins, *Goddess Worship, Witchcraft, and Other Neo-Pagan Movements.*

[117]Margot Adler, *Drawing Down the Moon* (Boston: Beacon Press, 1986), ix.

system that mirrored and provided the sacred underpinnings of patriarchy."[118]

(4) Geoffrey Parrinder also notes that in the literature of the witch hunts, none of the named demons or devils were given pagan names: "All the names of the personages recorded are Biblical, ecclesiastical, or fanciful. . . . But we never find the old pagan gods Thor or Woden, Loki or Grendel, or the trolls. Nor are there to be found traces of Druidic or Celtic gods, or those of prehistoric fertility cults."[119]

d. Other names used to refer to contemporary witchcraft include the *craft, paganism, neo-paganism, Gaia,* and *the goddess movement.*

e. Contemporary witchcraft is generally pacifistic, nature-worshiping, and often vegetarian or at least respectful of animal life. The contemporary witch seeks to be *one with* the world, rather than, like many satanists, to *overcome* the world and use it for self-gratification.

2. Witchcraft is condemned in the Bible.

a. Biblical references to witchcraft refer to practices of sorcery and were forbidden in Israel (Deut. 18:9–14), condemned by the prophets (Micah 5:12), and described as a damnable "work of the flesh" (Gal. 5:20).

b. Other terms related to witchcraft include divination (Ezek. 13:6–7; Deut. 18:11–12; Lev. 20:6, 27), astrology (Isa. 47:13), false prophesy (Jer. 14:14), magic (Gen. 41:8), spiritism (attempting communication with the dead; Deut. 18:11), and sorcery (Exod. 22:18; Acts 13:6–8).

c. Biblical references refer more to practices than to beliefs or worship.

3. Witchcraft is sometimes used as a literary device representing evil familiar to us in fairy tales and classic Disney movies.

4. Some self-styled satanists call themselves "witches" or "warlocks." Anton LaVey sometimes uses the term "witch" to describe "an enchantress, one who fascinates, rather than the Feminist/Wiccan revision of witch as healer and midwife."[120] In his opinion, satanism is superior to neo-pagan witchcraft: "Satanism is a blend of wit and logic; Wicca is humorless stupidity."[121]

---

[118]Tikva Frymer-Kensky, *In the Wake of the Goddesses: Women, Culture and the Biblical Transformation of Pagan Myth* (New York: Fawcett Columbine, 1992), vii.

[119]Parrinder, *Witchcraft: European and African,* 65.

[120]Barton, *The Secret Life of a Satanist,* 166.

[121]Interview, 5 August 1994.

5. One reason people often confuse this with satanism is that this kind of witchcraft is almost universally intolerant and critical of Christianity.[122]

Ronald Hutton sees this prevailing critical attitude in contemporary British witchcraft writings, consisting of "an intense and consistent hostility to the Christian church. The follies and deficiencies of this institution are regularly held up to ridicule and abuse."[123]

B. Paganism, Polytheism, and Idol Worship

1. Paganism

   a. Paganism, that is, religious belief or worship contrary to the true beliefs and worship of the Bible, is an extremely broad term covering all kinds of false belief.

   b. Paganism can include satanism but is not a specific enough concept for our discussion.

   c. This use of the term *pagan* should not be confused with how the term is sometimes used by contemporary witches as a synonym for witch, mentioned above.

2. Polytheism

   a. Polytheism is a belief in more than one god—sometimes hundreds, or even thousands of gods or goddesses.

   b. A satanist who believes in the actual existence of both God and Satan as equal and opposite "gods" would be a polytheist, but otherwise the term is too general for our discussion. Hinduism and Mormonism, for example, are polytheistic but not classified under our specific definition of *satanism*.

3. Idol worship

   a. Idol worship is a concept common to the Old and New Testaments and refers to the worship (through a physical representation) of any false god and is denounced throughout Scripture (Exod. 34:13–16; Jer. 16:11–21; Hos. 4:12–19; Rom. 1:21–25).

   b. The Bible prohibits worship through any physical representation of the one true God, Yahweh, the triune God of the Bible, Father, Son, and Holy Spirit (Exod. 20:1–5).

C. Psychic Phenomena, New Ageism, and Mere Magic

1. Psychic Phenomenon

   a. Psychic phenomenon is a general term referring to any magical practice that allegedly produces miraculous results or results not obtainable through natural physical laws.

   b. Such practices are condemned in Scripture (see above under Section I.A.2).

---

[122]Passantino and Passantino, *When the Devil Dares Your Kids*, 89.

[123]Hutton, *The Pagan Religions of the Ancient British Isles*, 336.

  c. While a satanist may engage in a practice said to produce psychic phenomena, many others such as witches, New Agers, and general occultists engage in such practices as well.

 2. New Ageism

  a. New Ageism refers to the beliefs, practices, or worldview of the New Age Movement.

  b. New Ageism, although also contrary to Scripture, is not the same as satanism.[124]

 3. "Mere" Magic

  a. "Mere" magic, mentalism, and stage magic refer to sleight of hand and other performance art where both practitioner and audience know the performance is done through various forms of trickery such as mis-direction, special effects, props, and the like.

  b. This is a form of entertainment and is not inherently connected to the occult.[125]

II. Misconceptions About Anton LaVey and the Church of Satan

A. *Origin*

 1. Many people think LaVey started the Church of Satan as a rival church or religion against Christianity.

 2. However, LaVey considers himself a humanistic iconoclast (one who overturns icons or sacred precepts of a culture or society in favor of individual human freedom) and actually is *opposed* to a structured, autocratic social system, even of satanism.[126]

B. *Worldview*

"LaVey describes Satanism as a secular philosophy of rationalism and self-preservation (natural law, animal state), gift wrapping these ideas in religious trappings to add to their appeal."[127]

C. *Practices*

 1. While LaVey "specifically *prohibits*: harming children; killing non-human animals except for food or in self-defense; telling your trou-

---

[124]See Ron Rhodes, *The New Age Movement*, in this series.

[125]See, for example, André Kole, *Miracles or Magic?* (Eugene, Oreg.: Harvest House, 1987). See also André Kole and Terry Holley, *Astrology and Psychic Phenomena*, in this series.

[126]"The idea behind starting the Church of Satan was not to gain millions of dependent souls who needed activities and organized weekly meetings to keep them involved. LaVey started an organization for non-joiners, the alienated few who felt disenfranchised because of their independence, and who pridefully adopted Satan, the original rebel, as their patron" (Barton, *The Secret Life of a Satanist*, 13).

[127]Ibid., 201.

bles or giving opinions unasked; and making sexual advances toward someone who may not appreciate it."

2. He also declares, "If a guest in your lair annoys you, treat him cruelly and without mercy," and "When walking in open territory, bother no one. If someone bothers you, ask him to stop. If he does not stop, destroy him."[128]

D. *Rumors*

LaVey does not have an adult son or daughter who has "escaped" his cult and seeks shelter from Christians. This rumor has been spread over the last fifteen years by a person claiming to be LaVey's offspring, but this story has been carefully checked, and it is not true.[129]

III. Misconceptions About Satanic Holidays

Some sensationalists distribute various "satanic calendars" that are supposed to provide authoritative documentation for the dozens of satanic holidays. However, there is no uniformly followed satanic calendar, although most satanists follow LaVey's five major holidays:[130]

A. *A Satanist's Birthday*

"The highest of all holidays in the Satanic religion is the date of one's own birth. . . . The Satanist feels: 'Why not really be honest and if you are going to create a god in your own image, why not create that god as yourself.' Every man is a god if he chooses to recognize himself as one."[131]

B. *The Spring Equinox (also called Walpurgisnacht)*

C. *The Fall Equinox (also called Halloween or All Hallows' Eve)*

D. *The Summer Solstice*

E. *The Winter Solstice*

IV. Misconceptions About Satanism and Popular Entertainment

A. *Verbal Content and Subliminal Messages*

1. Studies have failed to demonstrate any correlation between subliminal messages (including backward masking) and listeners' behaviors or beliefs.[132]

---

[128]Quoted from LaVey's "Eleven Rules of the Earth" in Barton, *The Secret Life of a Satanist*, 209.

[129]The investigator who checked the story has an in-depth article in preparation for publication as of the summer of 1994.

[130]LaVey, *The Satanic Bible*, 96–98.

[131]Ibid., 96.

[132]Passantino and Passantino, *When the Devil Dares Your Kids*, 219.

2. The verbal content of songs, movies, comic books, fantasy role-playing games, etc., do not cause changes in listeners' behaviors or beliefs; listeners choose verbal content consistent with or supportive of their behaviors and beliefs. Satanic lyrics do not cause satanists; rather, satanists enjoy satanic lyrics.[133]

3. Inappropriate messages through any medium can promote inappropriate actions, beliefs, and values such as sexual immorality, violence, or mockery of authority. However, that is not the same as attributing special demonic power to satanically themed media.

B. *Other Entertainment Myths*

1. Most entertainment forms targeted by sensationalist Christians are not within our narrow definition of the satanic, although they do represent values and worldviews opposed to Christianity.

2. Many entertainment figures whose lyrics, roles, or actions promote satanism or satanic images are not serious satanists, but use satanism as a commercial enhancement to their performances.

3. It is not true that a vast satanic conspiracy is infiltrating American society through covert media persuasion.

C. *Corporate Myths*

1. It is also not true that any major American corporation has appeared in any public forum espousing satanism or admitting support or financial contributions to any satanic group.[134]

2. This satanic "myth" has been popularized over the last twenty years in several versions. The most enduring version is that the president of Proctor and Gamble appeared on the Phil Donahue television program and admitted he was a member of the Church of Satan and supported that church financially. There is not a shred of evidence for this, and Christians who propagate such stories damage the credibility of legitimate warnings regarding false belief.

V. Misconceptions About Satanism and Criminal Activity[135]

A. *Satanic Crime Versus Crime Committed by Satanists*

1. One must distinguish between crimes that are a result or requirement of a religion and crimes that are committed by adherents of a religion. In the case of satanism, one must distinguish between crimes that are a result or requirement of one's particular brand of satanism and crimes that are committed by people who happen to be satanists.

---

[133]Ibid., 105–29, see especially 119, 213–14.

[134]Further information on satanism and the media is in ibid., 105–29.

[135]Greater detail on crimes associated with satanism and satanists is available in ibid., 131–60.

2. There are no known public satanist organizations that advocate criminal activity.

3. However, the general self-indulgent, antinomian (i.e., "without law") satanic belief system could be compatible with criminal activity as long as the individual satanist were willing to risk the consequences.

4. Therefore we should not be surprised that some crimes are committed by satanists.

B. *Satanic crime is not a special classification of crime unlike any other illegal behavior. Rather, satanic crime is ordinary crime committed by criminals who are committed to a satanic worldview.*

C. *Satanic crime and the behaviors associated with satanic crime are more indicators of the perpetrator's serious social and moral problems than are the satanic beliefs by themselves.*

D. *Incidence Rate of Satanic Crime*

1. While the incidence rate of satanic crime is nowhere near the sensationalistic proportions reported by tabloid media (both broadcast and print), it is probably significantly higher than court records show.

2. The primary reason for under-reporting is that the satanic elements of the crimes do not add materially to the evidence proving the crime or the perpetrator. That is, the presence of occult signs at a crime scene or in a suspect's home are not considered integral to the crime itself, any more than finding a Catholic saint's medal dropped by a bank robber would implicate the Catholic church.

3. A second reason for under-reporting is that some prosecutors, aware of the sensationalism some attach to satanism, believe the introduction of marginally related occult aspects can harm their cases' credibility.

4. Third, many law enforcement personnel discount satanic beliefs and ignore them when they are held by a suspect or are in some way involved in the commission of a crime.

5. Fourth, there are so many spurious reports that have been shown to be false that some law enforcement personnel and prosecutors are reluctant to focus on the satanic aspects of a case they are investigating or prosecuting.

E. *When people who are also satanists engage in criminal activity, the following are the most prevalent kinds of crimes they commit:*

1. Drug dealing or drug use are common among teenage satanists. In fact, almost every teenage satanist we have interviewed or researched has used drugs.

2. Teenagers whose satanic involvement reflects personal problems may also be susceptible to suicide. Sometimes this is reflected in a boyfriend-girlfriend suicide pact.

3. Criminals who are also satanists often use satanic symbols or rituals during the commission of crimes (e.g., teenage satanist vandals, rather than spray painting a gang symbol on a bus stop, may spray paint a satanic symbol on a church wall).

4. Some sociopathic criminals such as some serial killers are dedicated, self-styled satanists, such as California serial killer Richard Ramirez.

5. Specific crimes associated with satanism are listed in *When the Devil Dares Your Kids*.

VI. Satanic Ritual Abuse (SRA)[136]

A. The Rise of SRA Stories

1. Stories about satanic ritual abuse (SRA) and generational satanism have become rampant in North America beginning in the late 1980s. While the proponents of these theories and the thousands of (mostly female) people who believe they are victims are sincere in their convictions, there is no more truth to SRA and generational satanism than there was to the great witch hunt theories of long ago.

2. The only material supportive of the stories are the unsubstantiated personal testimony accounts of persons who, in almost every case, have been strongly influenced by popular media sensationalism, therapeutic fads, and/or irresponsible and inaccurate journalism.

3. Therapeutic fads are the greatest factors in promoting SRA.

   They include dubious theories of repressed memories, recovered memories (especially those obtained through directive therapy, hypnosis, and chemical intervention), dissociative disorders (especially multiple personality disorder—MPD), post-traumatic stress syndrome (PTSS) applied to early childhood abuse, and directive support groups.

4. Some true believers in this phenomenon say that there are more than 100,000 "adult survivors" who have entered therapy and "remembered" these horrible abuses. Others more than double the number.[137]

5. True believers say the conspiracy is almost invincible, covers the nation (if not the world), and involves key power players in the courts, education, politics, religion, and society.[138]

---

[136]This issue is comprehensively analyzed in Bob Passantino and Gretchen Passantino, "The Hard Facts about Satanic Ritual Abuse," *Christian Research Journal* (Winter 1992): 21–34; and in their "Satanic Ritual Abuse in Popular Christian Literature," *Journal of Psychology and Theology*, 20, no.3 (1992): 299–305. This section uses material from both articles. Documentation for each of the statements in this section is in the two articles as well. Both articles are available in *The Occult Watch Pack*, which can be ordered from Answers In Action, P.O. Box 2067, Costa Mesa, CA 92628, or telephone (714) 646–9042.

[137]See Passantino and Passantino, "The Hard Facts about Satanic Ritual Abuse," for documentation.

[138]See Jerry Johnston, *The Edge of Evil*, which repeatedly assumes the validity of this massive, nearly undetectable, almost invincible satanic conspiracy. Johnston and others, for example, frequently repeat the undocumented speculation of Dr. Al Carlisle of the Utah State Prison System that between 40,000 and 60,000

B. SRA and the Law

1. True believers[139] provide unconditional support to alleged adult survivors whose therapeutically recovered "memories" typically indict their elderly parents for heinous crimes including murder, cannibalism, sexual torture, incest, and bestiality.

2. Some SRA "victims" seek legal recourse against their "abusers."

    a. Some bring their cases to law enforcement, hoping for criminal prosecution.

    b. Some obtain restraining orders barring their parents from seeing them or their grandchildren.

    c. Some cut all ties with family and disappear.

    d. Many file civil suits against their parents to recover damages and pay for anticipated lifelong therapy. Almost all are in the midst of long-term intensive therapeutic counseling; many are involved in dozens of psychiatric hospitalizations and almost daily therapy sessions and support group meetings.

    e. Small children are sometimes snatched from their parents' custody on the whisper of a suspicion that one or both parents may be involved in satanic ritual abuse.

3. True believers among therapists, alleged adult survivors, law enforcement, journalists, and Christian leaders call for everyone to believe the stories, to change the justice system so recovered "memories" alone can convict in criminal court, and to contend against this nearly invincible satanic conspiracy.[140]

C. Social Factors Leading to the Acceptance of SRA Stories

Four social factors arising during the 1970s and 1980s have fostered acceptance of SRA accounts.

1. Family disintegration

    a. Cohabitation and divorce rates climbed sharply, producing fragmented family units, single-parent families, blended families, and many children without consistent, caring adult involvement.

---

persons per year are ritually murdered. Another example is Cory Hammond, therapist and popular SRA seminar leader, who teaches that satanic mind control was developed in a mutually benefiting conspiracy among the United States Government, former Nazi researchers, and the satanic hierarchy.

[139]"True believer" is used in this context to refer to someone who is sincerely committed to believing the SRA conspiracy worldview and who often is an outspoken proponent, such as a true believer therapist, law enforcement person, parent, adult survivor, and so on. While the true believer sincerely believes, that belief is not accurate and is a reflection of one's presuppositions regarding SRA rather than a reflection of the evidence, which is nonexistent.

[140]These themes are found in most of the literature, such as Daniel Ryder, *Breaking the Circle of Satanic Ritual Abuse* (Minneapolis: CompCare Publishers, 1992); James Friesen, *Uncovering the Mystery of MPD* (San Bernardino, Calif.: Here's Life, 1991), and Ellen Bass and Laura Davis', *The Courage to Heal* (New York: HarperCollins, 1992). The themes are promoted aggressively by many of the true-believer advocacy groups such as the Los Angeles County Ritual Abuse Task Force, Monarch Resources, and JUSTUS Unlimited.

53

    b. This led to more serious social and emotional problems, including incest in blended families and antisocial behavior among adolescents.

    c. This also led to a significant rise in child custody, abandonment, and neglect as well as accusations of such problems.

2. Mental health community

    a. The mental health community expanded its ranks and gained significant social acceptance, increasing the impact of any diagnosis or treatment mistakes.

    b. Many people (including many mental health professionals themselves) came to trust the mental health community to be uniformly competent in the three areas of investigation, diagnosis, and treatment.

    c. It expanded its ranks past traditionally educated, credentialed, and regulated psychiatrists and psychologists to include many different kinds of counselors, including licensed therapists, social workers, lay counselors, peer counselors, support group members and leaders, and pastoral counselors. These many different kinds of counselors have varying degrees of education prerequisites, credentialing standards, and regulatory accountability.

3. Activism against pornography and child abuse

    a. Heightened concern in these areas created a vulnerability to over-reporting, over-diagnosis, and credulous acceptance of unproven assertions that fit the pornography-abuse model.

    b. The special interest groups' assertions could not be tested until a comprehensive database of research could be accumulated. This had the effect of allowing these errors to go unchecked.

    c. Less credible groups and "experts" needed to promote a danger of sufficient depth and breadth to warrant large commitments of time, legislation, and funding.

4. Popular expectations

    a. Both the secular media and the evangelical media responded to people's increasing interest in sensationalism.

    b. American evangelicalism, with its growing interest in "end times" speculation, expected a growing atmosphere of spiritual wickedness leading up to the imminent rapture of the church (one interpretation of Matthew 24). This corresponded to stories of satanic conspiracies and SRA.

    c. Tabloid media (both broadcast and print) lowered media standards of investigative fact-finding and reporting and also gave platforms to undocumentable personal claims.

D. The Typical SRA Story

The typical SRA story displays uniform essential elements, whether or not the story is "discovered" by a therapist, social worker, or parent and whether or not the victim is an adult or a child.

1. The victims

   a. The common adult victim is a white woman between the ages of twenty-five and forty-five with a previous history of nonspecific psychological problems, often a history of suicide attempts, and who is either intensely religious (usually evangelical or charismatic Protestant) or comes from an intensely religious background or exposure.

   b. The typical adult victim is highly suggestible, intelligent, creative, and well-learned if not well-educated.

   c. The victim first seeks counseling help for a seemingly unrelated problem.

   d. Victims typically believe the truth of their story.

   From our own conversations with dozens of alleged adult survivors, we feel comfortable in affirming that the vast majority of them sincerely believe their stories, although sincerity cannot determine a story's veracity.

   e. Child victims present a somewhat different profile.

      (1) There is not one "common" child victim profile, although most are well-motivated to please adults, intelligent, and loyal to the supportive parent. Perhaps this is because children's disclosures of SRA almost always follow questioning by worried parents or mental health workers.

      (2) Often the supportive parent has characteristics in common with the typical adult victim.

      (3) If the child is disclosing SRA caused by an immediate family member, it is typically in a divorce or separation situation where the accused is the nonsupportive parent or one of the nonsupportive parent's relatives.

2. The victimizers

   a. Typically the victim's immediate family members are said to be the perpetrators (even if the victim may see the family as former victims who have turned to victimization because of their own trauma).

   b. When the immediate family is not involved (as in many of the children's stories but in almost none of the alleged adult survivor stories), care-givers in regular custody of the victim are accused as the perpetrators (preschool teachers, day-care workers, parents in divorce situations).

    c. The *hypothetical* psychological profile of the SRA perpetrator contradicts the most common features of *known* physical and sexual abusers, psychotics, sociopaths, pornographers, and serial killers, raising doubts whether such an abuser exists.

3. SRA characteristics

    a. The abuse includes emotional (terrifying threats, deliberate heightening of fear), physical (beating, cutting), sexual (incest, mutilation of sexual organs), and spiritual (threats that God won't forgive, Jesus is defeated) aspects.

    b. The ritual elements of the abuse are always satanic or occultic. Features of satanic ceremony folklore such as the Black Mass, human sacrifice, drinking of blood, and satanic symbols are common, although victims typically cannot reproduce the intricacies of occult ritual beyond what is commonly available through general media or what they have heard from other victims or therapists.

4. SRA disclosure

    a. Adult SRA stories

        (1) Usually adult SRA stories are disclosed in a therapeutic setting. With sensationalistic reports of SRA scattered throughout the media, there is hardly a client or therapist who has not heard SRA stories.

        (2) The adult victim generally begins therapy for a seemingly unrelated problem such as a sleep or eating disorder, depression, or marital difficulties. During the course of treatment either the therapist or the client will raise the possibility of repressed memories of SRA.

        (3) At first the client may deny a past history of SRA or may not remember anything or may have fragments of almost meaningless images of SRA. After long-term, intensive therapy with a therapist committed to believing the client no matter what, the alleged adult survivor and therapist will gradually piece together a complex personal SRA history.

        (4) Usually the therapist decides that the repression was facilitated by a dissociative state, multiple personality disorder (MPD).

        (5) After more long-term, intensive therapy and support group involvement, including "abreacting," or "reliving" each of the traumatic "memories," the client may become emotionally well.

    b. Child SRA stories

        (1) The child who discloses an SRA story almost always does so at the prompting of a parent or mental health professional.

        (2) Usually such disclosure comes after frequent, prolonged questioning.

(3) Usually the perpetrator is identified by the child as a nonfamily, regular care-giver such as a day-care worker.

(4) When family members are accused, they are most likely grandparents of the spouse other than the one reporting the abuse, or a parent or stepparent estranged from the family.

(5) Accusations against public officials, entertainment personalities, neighbors, or other more distant adults usually come only after the case has been sensationalized and the child has been questioned incessantly about "the others."

(6) Children are much less likely to be diagnosed with MPD. The common presumption is that they are terrified to tell, not that they have repressed their memories of SRA.

E. SRA as a Conspiracy

1. The common SRA story includes strong commitment to a conspiracy theory of history.

2. The victimization is not seen as the isolated, depraved action of a psychotic or sociopathic person. Instead, the victimization is part of a widespread, multigenerational, nearly omnipotent satanic conspiracy involving thousands or even millions of people, many in the highest levels of society, government, law enforcement, religion, and even mental health institutions.

3. When SRA stories first surfaced in the early 1980s, first with *Michelle Remembers* and then in 1983 with the McMartin preschool case in Southern California, followed by cases in Bakersfield, California, and Jordan, Minnesota, many journalists, law enforcement personnel, and mental health professionals tended to believe that SRA existed, at least hypothetically.

4. When dozens of stories turned into hundreds and then thousands of stories, none of which produced a single piece of corroborative evidence, some former believers became healthy skeptics.

   a. San Francisco police officer Sandi Gallant has qualified her former credulity, saying, "Our largest problem is that we live in a negative environment that breeds negative behavior [and] has little to do with spiritual beliefs."

   b. Supervisory Special Agent Kenneth Lanning of the FBI's Behavioral Science Unit has investigated more than 300 SRA reports and has yet to find corroborative evidence.

   While still affirming his willingness to look for and find such hypothetical evidence, Lanning points out the problems inherent in the SRA conspiracy theory: Any professional evaluating victims' allegations of ritualistic abuse cannot ignore the lack of physical evidence (no bodies or physical evidence left by violent murders), the difficulty in successfully committing a large-scale conspiracy crime (the more people involved in any crime conspiracy, the harder it is to get away with it), and human nature (intragroup conflicts resulting in individual self-serving disclosures are likely to occur in any group involved in organized kidnapping, baby breeding, and human sacrifice).

F. *Summary of Arguments Offered by True Believers for the Existence of SRA*

1. All conspiracies are secret and unknown.
2. Evidence *against* a story is evidence that a satanist planted false evidence.
3. Only a conspiracy such as true believers describe has the capability of destroying all the evidence.
4. The very people who should be fighting this but who criticize true believers as sensationalists are actually secret satanists themselves.
5. Only therapists can discern that victims are telling the truth.
6. Children (whether physiologically children or the fractured child personalities of an MPD client) don't lie about such horrible things, and no one would make up these horrific tales.
7. Accused perpetrators' refusal to confess shows the depths of depravity to which they have descended.
8. Nondeterminative evidence validates the conspiracy. For example, what a true believer calls a scar resulting from ritual abuse a skeptic calls an appendix operation scar.
9. Individual occult-related criminal acts validate the conspiracy.
10. The conspiracy explains the abduction of thousands of children each year.

G. *Fallacies in Arguments Offered by True Believers in SRA*

Logical examination of each of the above ten "proofs" quickly reveals fatal flaws in each of them.

1. No large-scale conspiracy can suppress all the evidence.
   a. While conspiracies are certainly secret, they cannot continue to exist and function in society without leaving a trail.
   b. For example, the FBI may not have known how extensive the Mafia's network was until years of painstaking investigation and the confessions of some members, but the Mafia left plenty of physical evidence in the form of bodies, bullet holes, arson cases, beatings, and a host of other illegal activities.
   c. Statistically, such an invincible secrecy is impossible.
   Suppose there are 100,000 adult survivors, representing only a small subgroup of the conspiracy. They are the ones who were not killed, who eventually escaped the control of the cult, who got into therapy, who "remembered" their abuse, and who then were will-

ing to tell about it. If we gauge the average number of abusive events per survivor at fifty (a conservative figure), we are confronted with 5,000,000 criminal events over the last fifty years in America alone—without a shred of corroborative evidence.

2. Evidence against a story is not evidence for a story.

   a. Evidence *against* a story, if gathered professionally and examined objectively, is just that: *evidence against* a story, not evidence *for* the story.

   b. Offering only one explanation for contrary evidence is committing an either-or (disjunctive) fallacy.

   c. Without evidence, suspicions of tampering with the evidence are groundless.

3. Lack of evidence is not proof of a story.

   a. The third argument, a variation on the second, falls into the same either-or fallacy: the true believer admits only one possible reason there is *no* evidence—obviously, only a conspiracy as big as the SRA stories could destroy everything. However, in reality there are at least two possible reasons there is no evidence, and one is that the theory is not true.

   b. The facts of the case do not change, but one's presupposition determines how the nonevidence will be interpreted. This is not a proof and certainly not evidence; it is a subjective belief.

4. It is paranoia to assume automatically that those who disagree are co-conspirators. Without some warrant for such charges, it dwindles to paranoid name-calling.

5. The notion that only therapists can tell when victims are telling the truth betrays a naive and inappropriate trust in authority in general and in the efficacy of psychotherapy in particular. It also illustrates a considerable degree of self-aggrandizement on the part of true-believer therapists.

6. Children do not always tell the truth.

   a. The idea that children (or childlike MPD manifestations) don't lie about abuse gained popularity during the early 1980s as part of the child protection movement. However, as much as we need to protect children from abuse, experts recognize today that, for a variety of reasons, children do not always tell the truth.[141]

   b. Such a fallacy of credulity on the part of true believers ignores both the complexity of possible reasons one could believe or tell a story that is not true and also the reality that some SRA stories have been shown to be false.

---

[141]See, for example, Lee Coleman, "False Allegations of Child Sexual Abuse," *Forum* (January-February 1986): 12–22.

7. Denial does not prove guilt.
   a. Accused perpetrators are given a nonlethal form of the same kind of guilt-or-innocence test given to suspected witches during the witch hunts: If the witch, once charged, didn't confess, that proved he or she was unrepentant and should die; if one did confess, the rightly deserved punishment was death.
   b. Today's true believers don't kill those they accuse, but they leave them with no way to affirm their innocence—a protestation of innocence becomes a tautological "proof" of guilt.
8. Nondeterminative evidence does not validate the conspiracy.
   a. True believers sometimes attempt to find corroborative evidence. Often they refer to amorphous "files full of evidence," but are unable to cite any single piece of evidence.
   b. Sometimes they refer to always unidentified "officials" who have seen their evidence and advised the victims to keep quiet or risk death from the avenging cult.[142]
9. Individual occult-related crime is no proof of SRA.
   a. True believers almost invariably point to sensationalistic crimes of great tragedy and violence as though they prove the SRA conspiracy. However, such crimes have little in common with the SRA phenomenon.
   b. For example, loner and self-styled satanist Richard Ramirez, convicted of multiple murder-robberies, had no association with any other satanists or satanic organizations or churches. He did not come from a family that practiced satanism and is considered to be a lone sociopathic serial killer.
   c. Sean Sellers, a self-styled teenaged satanist, involved in drugs and sex as well as his own brand of satanism, killed his parents because he was upset that they wanted him to break up with his girlfriend. Although he was personally committed to a satanic worldview, he was not part of any conspiracy.
   d. Ricky Kasso was a teenaged drug dealer and self-styled satanist who killed a friend during a satanic ritual in revenge for a drug deal gone bad. Kasso was initiated into satanism by an adult acquaintance, and Kasso brought a few of his friends into his rituals as well, but he was not part of any SRA-type satanic organization or "family."
   e. The Matamoros drug-smuggling ring killed several people to protect its drug trade, and some of the lower members of the ring were threatened through a combination of Roman Catholicism and African-Caribbean occultism called Palo Mayombe, but it was not related to any SRA conspiracy theories.

---

[142]See, for example, Ryder, *Breaking the Circle*, 99–106.

10. The statistics on missing children actually disprove SRA.

    a. The last support most true believers use is some variation on the idea that the SRA conspiracy explains a number of socially accepted ideas, signified here with the example of the commonly held assumption that there are thousands of missing children each year. The SRA conspiracy theory accounts for this phenomenon: the children are sacrificed in satanic rituals! Yet, when statistical studies are done concerning missing children, we find the truth does not fit the SRA conspiracy model.

    b. The vast majority of children reported missing each year are accounted for within a twelve-month period, leaving fewer than three hundred unaccounted for after one year.[143]

    The majority of missing children either are taken by noncustodial parents in custody disputes or are runaways. To a parent whose child is missing, the size of the problem is immaterial, the grief is real, and the suffering is deep. But it is wrong to confuse compassion for a person with a blind acceptance of false statistics in a futile effort to support an SRA conspiracy theory.

H. Rejection of SRA by Former True Believers

1. Many who at one time believed the SRA conspiracy theories have given up their theories because of a lack of evidence.

2. On the contrary, there is abundant evidence that this is a harmful social legend akin to the witch hunts.

3. Professionals in law enforcement, journalism, Christian counter-cult work, and mental health have recognized the deficiencies of the SRA model.[144]

4. Additionally, many who claim to have been falsely accused are working toward legal parity, reconciliation with their accusing family members, public exoneration, and reparation from therapists they believe have harmed them and their accusing family members with inappropriate therapy.

    a. Many who once believed they were victims of SRA have now recanted their stories and are working to help others, to reconcile with their families, and to call for accountability from their therapists.

    b. Professionals, recanters, and those who believe that they have been falsely accused have formed a nonprofit support and informational organization called the False Memory Syndrome Foundation, which has logged close to 20,000 reports.[145]

---

[143]Joel Best, "Missing Children, Misleading Statistics," *The Public Interest* 3 (1989): 84–92.

[144]For example, Police Sergeant Randy Emon, journalists Ethan Watters and Lawrence Wright, sociologist Dr. Richard Ofshe, and forensic psychologist Martha Rogers

[145]False Memory Syndrome Foundation, 3401 Market Street, Suite 130, Philadelphia, PA 19104–3315, or telephone (215) 387–1865.

Part IV: Theology

I. Preliminary Observations

A. *Use of Scripture*

  1. Scripture is the standard of belief for Christians. Since satanists reject Scripture, other kinds of arguments may be more meaningful to them, removing obstacles to their belief in Scripture and their reception of the gospel.

  2. In this section we provide scriptural answers to satanic teachings as the foundation for Christians, and other kinds of answers to satanic teachings that are meaningful to satanists, who reject the authority of Scripture.

B. *Satanic View*

  1. By "satanic view" in these sections we mean the views held or espoused by satanists. Because satanism is individualistic and iconoclastic, there are very few views that are articulated and supported by almost all satanists.

  2. The views presented in these sections are (a) held by LaVey and/or other leading satanists; (b) common among most satanists; or (c) are the most popularly recognized among satanists. For the most part they are summarized from various individual interview sources and are consequently not footnoted.

C. *Lack of Theological Distinctions*

  1. Satanists do not care enough about Christian theology to articulate specific opinions about specific theological positions.

  2. Satanists have such fundamental ignorance and misunderstanding in matters of basic Christian belief that it would take several additional book-length treatments to provide comprehensive answers. Consequently, in each of the refutation sections we provide general answers and then direct the reader to other books pertinent to the topic.

II. The Doctrine of Scripture

A. *The Satanist View of Scripture Briefly Stated*

Satanists reject the Christian Scripture and do not hold any book, including *The Satanic Bible*, as authoritative, revealed, or inspired.

B. *Arguments Used by Satanists to Defend Their View of Scripture*

Arguments from satanists focus not only on the Christian Bible but also on satanic writings, including *The Satanic Bible*.

1. *The Satanic Bible* written by Anton LaVey is not meant to be a "revelation" or "inspired" or "divine." It is his declaration of emancipation from the strictures of *any* organized, autocratic, centrally ordered system. It might be useful as a guide, but it is not something that must be obeyed or believed.

2. LaVey wrote *The Satanic Bible* on two levels: (1) As an open mockery of Christianity that draws many people who have rejected Christianity; and (2) On a more subtle level as a declaration of the supremacy of the truly enlightened, autonomous minority who recognize their natural superiority to the mass of lower humanity.

3. Since most satanists reject the existence of God (and therefore the supernatural), they necessarily reject the inspiration and authority of the Bible. They believe that the Bible is full of contradictions and in no way reflects truth about God, mankind, or human destiny.[146]

4. The Bible represents the worst in human enslavement to arbitrary, mythological, untrue superstitions designed to encourage "drone" behavior and to discourage independent, creative behavior.

C. *A Refutation of Satanist Arguments Regarding Scripture*

1. *The Satanic Bible*'s disdain for authority is self-refuting.

   a. At the same time that *The Satanic Bible* disclaims authority over others, it promotes its own philosophy of self as the highest, most personally liberating philosophy. Those who want to be the best should do and be the best, which *The Satanic Bible* says includes individual autonomy and self-interest.

   b. However, if *The Satanic Bible* presents an authoritative blueprint for the self-fulfilled life, but the self-fulfilled life includes refusal to acknowledge the authority of anything (including, presumably, *The Satanic Bible*) outside the self, then the satanist must wrestle with the quandry of obeying *The Satanic Bible* to achieve fulfillment while at the same time rejecting *The Satanic Bible* as an external authority.

2. Persuading satanists that God exists and that therefore the supernatural is possible opens the way for persuading them that the Bible is a supernatural communication from God.

   a. The existence of God is discussed below under Section III.

   b. Various evidences and arguments can be used within that framework for affirming that the Bible is God's revelation of truth and is free from contradiction or error.

   c. General arguments for the revelation truth-claims of the Bible are available in books such as Norman L. Geisler and William E. Nix, *General Introduction to the Bible*, 2d ed. (Chicago: Moody Press, 1992); Merrill C. Tenney, *The Bible: The Living Word of Revelation*

---

[146]LaVey, *The Satanic Bible*, 43.

(Grand Rapids: Zondervan, 1968); or René Pache, *The Inspiration and Authority of Scripture* (Chicago: Moody Press, 1969).

   d. Alleged Bible contradictions are discussed and reconciled in several good books, including Gleason Archer, *Encyclopedia of Bible Difficulties* (Grand Rapids: Zondervan, 1982); William Arndt, *Bible Difficulties and Seeming Contradictions* (1926; repr. St. Louis: Concordia, 1987); John Haley, *Alleged Discrepancies of the Bible* (1874; repr. Grand Rapids: Baker, 1984); and David E. O'Brien, *Today's Handbook for Solving Bible Difficulties* (Minneapolis: Bethany House, 1990).

3. Very few satanists who believe the Bible "represents the worst in human enslavement" have ever read the Bible. Usually their opinions arise from ignorance.

   a. Encouraging satanists to read the Bible with an open mind can be productive, especially if the satanist is shown passages that affirm the personal fulfillment God grants to those who are reconciled to him.

   b. Satanists who learn to understand the Bible in its cultural, historical, and literary context will find it to affirm human fulfillment according to the way we were designed by our Creator. Books on how to understand Scripture include Gordon D. Fee and Douglas Stuart, *How to Read the Bible for All Its Worth*, 2d ed. (Grand Rapids: Zondervan, 1993); Leland Ryken, *Words of Delight: A Literary Introduction to the Bible* (Grand Rapids: Baker, 1987); and Dan McCartney and Charles Clayton, *Let the Reader Understand: A Guide to Interpreting and Applying the Bible* (Wheaton, Ill.: Victor Books, 1994).

D. The Biblical Position Regarding Scripture

1. The Bible testifies to Jesus Christ, who alone grants eternal life.

   John 5:39 says, "You diligently study the Scriptures because you think that by them you possess eternal life. These are the Scriptures that testify about me, yet you refuse to come to me to have life."

2. The truth displayed through Scripture is not burdensome or enslaving, but instead provides mankind with all that is necessary for righteousness.

   Psalm 1:1–2 promises, "Blessed is the man who does not walk in the counsel of the wicked or stand in the way of sinners or sit in the seat of mockers. But his delight is in the law of the LORD, and on his law he meditates day and night."

3. The Bible judges mankind, even people's thoughts and attitudes.

   Hebrews 4:12 warns, "The word of God is living and active. Sharper than any double-edged sword, it penetrates even to dividing soul and spirit, joints and marrow; it judges the thoughts and attitudes of the heart."

4. The Bible is God's perfect Word, the source of spiritual life and health. Paul commends Timothy for knowing God's Word "from infancy" because it is "able to make you wise for salvation through faith in Christ Jesus." Paul explains, "All Scripture is God-breathed and is useful for teaching, rebuking, correcting and training in righteousness, so that the man of God may be thoroughly equipped for every good work" (2 Tim. 3:15–17).

5. Satanists reject the authority of Scripture, so they are unconcerned about the claims Scripture makes for itself. However, reasonable dialogue with satanists concerning Scripture should include the following:

   a. The authenticity and historicity of the Bibles we have today

   b. The revelatory power of God in human history

   c. The absolute standard of God's truth and righteousness as expressed in Scripture contrasted to their relativistic and subjective "truth" and individualistic morality

   d. The importance of seeking truth and testing those who claim to possess transcendent truth

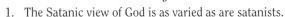

III. The Doctrine of God

A. *The Satanist View of God Briefly Stated*

1. The Satanic view of God is as varied as are satanists.

2. Most satanists do not believe in the existence of God at all.

3. Most of those who do affirm the existence of God identify God as some natural but nonmaterial force in the universe that can be used by humans.

B. *Arguments Used by Satanists in Support of Their View of God*

Arguments from satanists concerning God generally follow those of atheists or secular humanists.

1. LaVey biographer Burton H. Wolfe summarizes the satanic "theology":

   "There is no God. There is no supreme, all-powerful deity in the heavens that cares about the lives of human beings. There is nobody up there who gives a sh—. Man is the only god. Man must be taught to answer to himself and other men for his actions."[147]

2. God is the natural force of nature that can be used by anyone for his or her own goals.

   LaVey explains, "It is a popular misconception that the Satanist does not believe in God. The concept of 'God,' as interpreted by man, has been so varied throughout the ages, that the Satanist simply accepts the definition which suits him best. Man has always created his gods,

---

[147]Burton H. Wolfe, *The Devil's Avenger* (New York: Pyramid Books, 1974), 35.

rather than his gods creating him. God is, to some, benign—to others, terrifying. To the Satanist 'God'—by whatever name he is called, or by no name at all—is seen as the balancing force in nature, and not as being concerned with suffering. This powerful force which permeates and balances the universe is far too impersonal to care about the happiness or misery of flesh-and-blood creatures on this ball of dirt upon which we live."[148]

3. God is the self.

"I am a Satanist! Bow down, for I am the highest embodiment of human life!"[149]

C. Refutation of the Satanist View of God

1. The first problem with satanist views of God is that they do not understand what the Bible teaches about God.

   a. They think that the God of the Bible is like an anthropomorphic god out of Greek or Roman mythology; that he is cruel, arbitrary, egotistical, tyrannical, and demanding.

   b. The Bible describes God as eternal, nonmaterial, infinite, unchanging, all-knowing, and all-powerful. He is not like any kind of mythological god or the god of any other religious tradition.

   Books that discuss the nature and attributes of God from a philosophical perspective include Norman L. Geisler and Winfried Corduan, *Philosophy of Religion*, 2d. ed. (Grand Rapids: Zondervan, 1988); Geisler and William D. Watkins, *Worlds Apart* (Grand Rapids: Baker, 1989); Stuart Hackett, *The Reconstruction of the Christian Revelation Claim* (Grand Rapids: Baker, 1984) and *The Resurrection of Theism* (Grand Rapids: Baker, 1957).

   c. God's moral attributes are contrary to the satanists' mischaracterization of God.

   (1) God is just, merciful, and loving, and his ethics are absolute since they flow from his nature.

   (2) Books on explaining the biblical view of God, his moral attributes, and ethics include Norman L. Geisler, *Christian Ethics: Options and Issues* (Grand Rapids: Baker, 1989); Wayne Grudem, *Systematic Theology* (Grand Rapids: Zondervan, 1994); Walter R. Martin, *Essential Christianity* (Ventura, Calif.: Regal Books, 1975 ed.); and J. I. Packer, *Knowing God* (Downers Grove, Ill.: InterVarsity Press, 1973).

2. The second problem of satanists is that most do not accept the existence of God.

   Christians can talk to satanists who reject the existence of God in the same ways as with other atheists.

---

[148]LaVey, *The Satanic Bible*, 40.
[149]Ibid., 45.

a. Some reject the existence of God because they believe the existence of God is illogical.

b. Some believe that the only reality is the material world and since God is not material, he must not exist.

c. Some reject the existence of God because they believe any hypothetical God would be completely divorced from the material world of our existence and therefore his existence is meaningless.

d. Some believe it is impossible to know whether God exists, and therefore it is meaningless to talk about God or to attempt to discover his existence.

e. Each of these kinds of positions can be answered logically and persuasively, although it is beyond the scope of this volume to do so.

(1) Several of the excellent books on the existence of God include Norman L. Geisler and Winfried Corduan, *Philosophy of Religion*, 2d. ed. (Grand Rapids: Baker, 1988); J. P. Moreland, *Scaling the Secular City: A Defense of Christianity* (Grand Rapids: Baker, 1987); and Richard Purtill, *Reason to Believe* (Grand Rapids: Eerdmans, 1974).

(2) A good way to encourage an atheist to consider the existence of God is to give him a book that contains both the theistic and the atheistic viewpoints, such as J. P. Moreland and Kai Nielsen's debate, *Does God Exist? The Great Debate* (Nashville: Thomas Nelson, 1990).

3. When satanists are confronted with rational, critical arguments for the existence of the biblical God, they probably will be at a loss as to how to respond. Satanists believe that all Christians are ignorant fools who have silly "Santa Claus" ideas about some made-in-his-own-image God in the heavens. Rational discourse about the necessary existence of a transcendent, eternal, personal God will challenge satanists to rethink their opinions of Christian belief.

D. The Biblical Position Regarding God

1. Scripture says that all people inherently know that God exists and that their sin and rebelliousness cause them to deny God.

Romans 1:18–19 declares that wickedness is at the root of the denial of God: "The wrath of God is being revealed from heaven against all the godlessness and wickedness of men who suppress the truth by their wickedness, since what may be known about God is plain to them, because God has made it plain to them."

2. No one can claim ignorance of God's existence or eternal power.

"For since the creation of the world God's invisible qualities—his eternal power and divine nature—have been clearly seen, being understood from what has been made, so that men are without excuse" (Rom. 1:20).

3. Those who deny the truth about God may, like satanists, believe that they are superior to or more intelligent than others, but "although they knew God, they neither glorified him as God nor gave thanks to him, but their thinking became futile and their foolish hearts were darkened. Although they claimed to be wise, they became fools and exchanged the glory of the immortal God for images made to look like mortal man [to the satanist, this is himself] and birds and animals and reptiles" (Rom. 1:21–23).

4. Scripture denies that anyone can be "God," the Great "I am," and condemns any worship of the self.

God warns such idolators: "Now then, listen, you wanton creature, lounging in your security and saying to yourself, 'I AM, and there is none besides me. I will never be a widow or suffer the loss of children.' Both of these will overtake you in a moment, on a single day: loss of children and widowhood. They will come upon you in full measure, in spite of your many sorceries and all your potent spells. You have trusted in your wickedness and have said, 'No one sees me.' Your wisdom and knowledge mislead you when you say to yourself, 'I am, and there is none besides me.' Disaster will come upon you, and you will not know how to conjure it away" (Isa. 47:8–11).

IV. The Doctrine of Jesus Christ

A. *The Satanist View of Jesus Christ Briefly Stated*

Satanists either reject the historical existence of Christ altogether or view him as a religious failure whose death on the cross epitomized his victim mentality.

B. *Arguments Used by Satanists to Defend Their View of Jesus Christ*

1. Jesus Christ is only a mythological, nonhistorical figure. Historical and literary scholarship proves Jesus never existed.

2. Even if Jesus existed, he was a poor excuse for a human being.

The Satanic Bible declares, "I dip my forefinger in the watery blood of your impotent mad redeemer, and write over his thorn-torn brow: The TRUE prince of evil—the king of the slaves!"[150]

3. Christianity's Jesus Christ is the opposite of everything the satanist wants to be.

Who wants to emulate someone who wouldn't defend himself and who preached sentimental "love" instead of self-defense and personal power?

4. Jesus Christ is not the redeemer, in LaVey's terms: "Say unto thine own heart, 'I am mine own redeemer.'"[151]

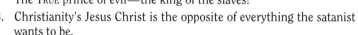

[150]Ibid., 30.
[151]Ibid., 33.

69

C. Refutation of the Satanist View of Jesus Christ

1. The historical existence of Jesus Christ and the historical and literary integrity of the New Testament are abundantly supported by archaeology, textual criticism, historical investigation, and literary criticism.

   a. Satanists who reject the historicity of Jesus Christ and the New Testament are ignorant of the facts.

   b. Some of the many books with good information on this subject include F. F. Bruce, *Jesus and Christian Origins Outside the New Testament* (Grand Rapids: Eerdmans, 1974); William L. Craig, *Knowing the Truth about the Resurrection* (Ann Arbor, Mich.: Servant Books, 1988); Gary R. Habermas, *Ancient Evidence for the Life of Jesus* (Nashville: Thomas Nelson, 1984); William H. Ramsay, *St. Paul: The Traveller and the Roman Citizen* (Grand Rapids: Baker, 1962); Paul Barnett, *Is the New Testament History?* (Ann Arbor, Mich.: Servant Books, 1986); Harry Boer, *The Bible and Higher Criticism* (Grand Rapids: Eerdmans, 1977); F. F. Bruce, *The Books and the Parchments* (Westwood, N.J.: Fleming H. Revell, 1963); and Gaalyah Cornfeld, *Archaeology of the Bible Book by Book* (New York: Harper & Row, 1976).

2. Those who think Christ's death on the cross is evidence that he was a spineless, foolish pacifist don't understand the altruistic significance of his death.

   A soldier who sacrifices his life to save his platoon is called a courageous hero, not a cowardly pacifist. Satanists have no conception of the meaning of Christ's death on the cross: his atoning sacrifice in payment for our sins to reconcile us to God. Just as the soldier saves his buddies by self-sacrifice, so Christ saves sinners by self-sacrifice.

3. Understanding Christ's person and work from Scripture clarifies his strong, assertive commitment to fulfilling God's redemptive purpose courageously with full knowledge that only his sacrifice was sufficient to pay the penalty for human sin.

   Some good books on the character and person of Christ include F. F. Bruce, *Jesus: Lord and Savior* (Downers Grove, Ill.: InterVarsity Press, 1986); Michael Griffiths, *The Example of Jesus* (Downers Grove, Ill.: InterVarsity Press, 1985); Everett F. Harrison, *A Short Life of Christ* (Grand Rapids: Eerdmans, 1968); and David F. Wells, *The Person of Christ* (Westchester, Ill.: Crossway Books, 1984).

4. Satanists who claim they are their own redeemers, assuming they mean this literally, are self-refuting.

   a. For someone to be a redeemer, one must have the substitute for the debt owed, whether it is the principal plus interest for a monetary debt or, as in this case, the sinless life for a sinful life.

   b. One who is in need of redemption from sin is, by definition, a sinner and therefore not qualified to be a redeemer. So if one is in need of a redeemer, one is obviously not qualified to be a redeemer oneself.

c. Several books provide good information on the nature of the atonement, including the classic by Archibald A. Hodge, *The Atonement* (1867; repr. Grand Rapids: Guardian Press, 1986); James Montgomery Boice, *God: The Redeemer* (Downers Grove, Ill.: InterVarsity Press, 1978); and Peter Toon, *Justification and Sanctification* (Westchester, Ill.: Crossway Books, 1983).

D. The Biblical Position Regarding Jesus Christ

1. The Bible clearly teaches that Jesus Christ is the Son of God who literally and historically was incarnated, lived, died, and was resurrected on our behalf.

   Peter affirmed, "We did not follow cleverly invented stories when we told you about the power and coming of our Lord Jesus Christ, but we were eyewitnesses of his majesty" (2 Peter 1:16).

2. Luke attests to the historicity of Christ as he opens his gospel:

   "Many have undertaken to draw up an account of the things that have been fulfilled among us, just as they were handed down to us by those who from the first were eyewitnesses and servants of the word. Therefore, since I myself have carefully investigated everything from the beginning, it seemed good also to me to write an orderly account for you, most excellent Theophilus, so that you may know the certainty of the things you have been taught" (Luke 1:1–4).

3. Paul argued before the government officials, "I am not insane.... What I am saying is true and reasonable. The king is familiar with these things, and I can speak freely to him. I am convinced that none of this has escaped his notice, because it was not done in a corner" (Acts 26:25–26).

4. The miserable, weak, ineffectual Jesus Christ described by satanists is not the Jesus Christ revealed in Scripture.

   The Jesus of Scripture healed the sick, rebuked the demonic, controlled the forces of nature, raised the dead, rebuked the hypocrites, sacrificed himself on behalf of sinful humanity, and ultimately will judge the world (including unrepentant satanists).

5. The power and majesty of Christ will be evident to all at the judgment.

   As John describes it prophetically, "I saw heaven standing open and there before me was a white horse, whose rider is called Faithful and True. With justice he judges and makes war. His eyes are like blazing fire, and on his head are many crowns. He has a name written on him that no one but he himself knows. He is dressed in a robe dipped in blood, and his name is the Word of God. The armies of heaven were following him, riding on white horses and dressed in fine linen, white and clean. Out of his mouth comes a sharp sword with which to strike down the nations. 'He will rule them with an iron scepter.' He treads the winepress of the fury of the wrath of God Almighty. On his robe and on his thigh he has this name written: KING OF KINGS AND LORD OF LORDS" (Rev. 19:11–16).

6. Whether or not satanists like it, the day will come when they, too, will acknowledge that salvation comes only from Jesus Christ (Acts 4:12) and that he alone is worthy to be called Lord:

"That at the name of Jesus every knee should bow, in heaven and on earth and under the earth, and every tongue confess that Jesus Christ is Lord, to the glory of God the Father" (Phil. 2:10–11).

V. The Doctrine Concerning Satan

A. Satanist Views of Satan Briefly Stated

1. Satanists vary in their views of Satan.

2. Some believe that the title refers to a natural, nonmaterial force (either neutral or "dark").

3. Some refer the title to themselves.

4. A few (usually self-taught teenagers from Christian backgrounds) are afraid he exists and is who the Bible says he is, but consider the power that comes from worshiping him worth a future hell.

B. Arguments Used by Satanists to Defend Their View of Satan

1. He is a neutral force used for personal gain.

a. He is "not the stereotyped fellow cloaked in red garb, with horns, tail and pitchfork, but rather the dark forces in nature that human beings are just beginning to fathom."[152]

b. "He merely represents a force of nature—the powers of darkness which have been named just that because no religion has taken these forces out of the darkness. Nor has science been able to apply technical terminology to this force. It is an untapped reservoir that few can make use of because they lack the ability [to take] advantage of this many faceted key to the unknown—which the Satanist chooses to call 'Satan.'"[153]

2. Many satanists identify themselves as Satan.

a. Because self-fulfillment, self-indulgence, and self-gratification are the goals of contemporary satanists, many satanists "worship" themselves and will identify themselves with the title "Satan" even though they do not believe in the actual existence of a spirit being named Satan.

b. Asked by a Christian whether he had ever seen or talked to Satan, one satanist pointed to himself and declared, "You're looking at Satan and talking to him right now!"

---

[152]Ibid., introduction by Burton H. Wolfe, 15.
[153]Ibid., 62.

C. A Refutation of Satanist Arguments Concerning Satan

1. The Bible clearly identifies Satan as an evil spirit in rebellion against God who seeks to draw humans away from salvation in Christ.

   a. This was shown in the beginning of the history section (see Part II, Section II).

   b. The satanists who acknowledge his evil and his power are closer to a scriptural understanding of satanic evil and may therefore be easier to approach than others.

   c. Books presenting basic biblical information about Satan include Michael Green, *I Believe in Satan's Downfall* (Grand Rapids: Eerdmans, 1981) and F. C. Jennings, *Satan: His Person, Work, Place, and Destiny* (Neptune, N.J.: Loizeaux Brothers, 1975). (See also the "For Further Reading" section of this book.)

2. Those satanists who believe that Satan is merely an anthropomorphism for "natural forces" or "dark natural forces" need not only to understand that Satan is a personal, evil spirit but also to reject dualism, or the idea that all of existence (including God) is a combination of good and evil.

   Helpful discussions of dualism are in Norman L. Geisler and Winfried Corduan, *Philosophy of Religion*, 2d. ed. (Grand Rapids: Baker, 1988) and Geisler and William D. Watkins, *Worlds Apart* (Grand Rapids: Baker, 1989).

3. Satanists who ascribe that title to themselves are subscribing to a form of humanism, or the belief that humankind as the highest form of life is accountable only to itself. A good Christian evaluation of contemporary humanism in Norman L. Geisler, *Is Man the Measure?* (Grand Rapids: Baker, 1983).

D. The Biblical View Concerning Satan

1. Evil is not natural. It is a result of personal rebellion against God not only by Satan but also by humankind (Rom. 5:12).

2. Those satanists who believe that Satan is a "neutral force" need to understand that there are no "neutral" spiritual or personal forces in the universe.

   Jesus proclaimed, "He who is not with me is against me, and he who does not gather with me scatters" (Matt. 12:30).

3. Satanists need to be told that the Bible prophesies that Satan and all his demons and followers will ultimately face judgment and eternal conscious separation from God's loving presence.

   "The devil, who deceived them, was thrown into the lake of burning sulfur, where the beast and the false prophet had been thrown. They will be tormented day and night for ever and ever" (Rev. 20:10).

73

VI. The Doctrine of Man

A. The Satanist View of Man Briefly Stated

Satanists who are intellectually sophisticated enough to consider the nature of man generally adopt a view that stratifies humans into two categories: the rational elite (the satanists) and those whom the rational elite exploit for their own gratification.

B. Arguments Used by Satanists to Defend Their View of Man

1. LaVey does not believe all humans are equal in value but rather that there are classes of humans superior to others.

   Asked his opinion of mankind, LaVey gives the pithy response, "For the one percent, admiration; for the rest, tolerance (at best)."[154]

2. Some humans are more enlightened and deserve more than others.

   LaVey designates this kind of human as the true satanist, "the small percentage of the population that he feels are chromosomally different, and perhaps chromosomally resistant to the effects of control. Stratification is a magical process of purification—subtractive rather than additive."[155]

3. Some humans are less enlightened and deserve nothing but contempt by the enlightened.

   LaVey has little patience with the "unenlightened" class of people: "I consider [helping the needy] a most ignoble endeavor.... It would be most merciful to help them by relieving them of the life they seem to hate so much. People should be happy I'm not a humanitarian—or I'd probably be the most diabolical mass murderer the world has ever known."[156]

4. The individual is supreme and is most fulfilled by self-indulgence, even at the expense of others.

5. The individual can have as much power as desired, accomplished through individual effort and the capitulation of others to one's superior demands.

6. There is no such thing as life or existence after death, although LaVey notes, "The only problem with having older friends is you have to see them all die off. It sure would be nice if there really was some place where you could see all your old friends again after you die."[157]

---

[154]Interview, 5 August 1994.

[155]Barton, *The Secret Life of a Satanist*, 211.

[156]Ibid., 133.

[157]Ibid., 74.

C. A Refutation of Satanist Views Concerning Man

1. The egocentric humanism embraced by satanists contradicts common assumptions in psychology, sociology, philosophy, and other academic disciplines concerning humanness.

   A good introduction to this subject is in Geisler's *Is Man the Measure?* (see Section V.C.3).

2. Egocentricism becomes a self-refuting view as soon as two or more egos are involved.

   a. The egocentric worldview holds that exploitation for one's self-gratification is "good."

   b. If this principle is extrapolated to apply to all individuals generally, however, then for every self-gratified person (a good state of affairs) there is an exploited one (a bad state of affairs). Consequently, the egocentric world cannot be the ideal one, since at least some people in this world fail to achieve self-gratification—the satanists' goal.

3. Satanists cannot account for Christians who can intelligently defend their faith.

   a. Satanists who are convinced they are in a superior mental or spiritual category because of their "enlightened" self-interest are confounded when they encounter Christians who believe the Bible but who (contradictorily, in the satanists' opinion) demonstrate careful, intelligent, rational ability and a firm understanding of reality.

   b. The Christian who takes satanist ideas seriously and attempts to respond to them genuinely, intelligently, and from a sound foundation in God's Word will contradict the satanists' opinion of their own superiority over all others, especially Christians.

D. The Biblical Position Regarding Man

1. Scripture clearly classifies all humans equally as far as their spiritual natures and created worth are concerned.

2. All humans are descended from the first humans God created—who were created perfect physically and spiritually (Gen. 1:26ff.).

3. All humans were represented by the first humans in their rebellion and consequently are deserving of death and God's eternal punishment (Rom. 3:23).

4. Humankind was rescued from universal eternal condemnation by God's loving action, not because some (or all) deserved God's grace (Rom. 5:6–8).

5. Christians are commanded to show love toward all, without favoritism and without personal boasting or self-interest (Phil. 2:1–4).

VII. The Doctrines of Sin and Salvation

A. *The Satanist View of Sin and Salvation Briefly Stated*

1. Satanists reject not only the actual biblical doctrines of sin and salvation, but also their own misrepresentation of the biblical doctrines.

2. Satanists reject the reality of sin and consequently see no need for salvation.

3. They believe instead that self-fulfillment is accomplished only through self-effort.

B. *Arguments Used by Satanists to Defend Their Views of Sin and Salvation*

1. Sin is an invention by Christianity to create "business" for itself.

   "To have the faintest stirring of sexual desire is to be guilty of lust. In order to insure the propagation of humanity, nature made lust the second most powerful instinct, the first being self-preservation. Realizing this, the Christian church made fornication the 'Original Sin.' In this way they made sure no one would escape sin. Your very state of being is a result of sin—the *Original* sin!"[158]

2. Humans cannot be "saved" by Christ's death on the cross.

   "Behold the crucifix; what does it symbolize? Pallid incompetence hanging on a tree."[159]

3. Human fulfillment is accomplished through human effort and power.

   a. Satanists do not look to any god or supernatural force to "save" them from their problems.

   b. LaVey's biographer, Blanche Barton, compares the satanist to the astute carnival magician who "knows there aren't any miracles— there is only what you make happen in life yourself."[160]

4. There is no judgment for one's actions, either in this life or after death (when one ceases to exist).

   LaVey proclaims, "There is no heaven of glory bright, and no hell where sinners roast. Here and now is our day of torment! Here and now is our day of joy! Here and now is our opportunity! Choose ye this day, this hour, for no redeemer liveth!"[161]

5. Reconciliation with God is the opposite of the satanic goal, that is, self-fulfillment through self-indulgence.

   LaVey discounts any value in prayer for forgiveness: "Just as the Satanist does not pray to God for assistance, he does not pray for forgiveness for his wrong-doings."[162]

---

[158] LaVey, *The Satanic Bible*, 47.

[159] Ibid., 31.

[160] Barton, *The Secret Life of a Satanist*, 42.

[161] LaVey, *The Satanic Bible*, 33.

[162] Ibid., 41.

C. A Refutation of Satanist Views Concerning Sin and Salvation

1. Satanists misrepresent the biblical doctrines of sin and salvation.

   a. The first step to refuting the satanist views of sin and salvation is to define clearly the biblical doctrines over against their misrepresentation by satanists.

   b. There are many good introductory doctrine or theology books that deal with these doctrines, including Alan F. Johnson and Robert E. Webber, *What Christians Believe: A Biblical and Historical Summary* (Grand Rapids: Zondervan, 1989); Alister E. McGrath, *Understanding Doctrine: What It Is—And Why It Matters* (Grand Rapids: Zondervan, 1990); and Walter Martin's small handbook, *Essential Christianity* (Ventura, Calif.: Regal, 1980).

   c. A second step in refuting the satanist views of sin and salvation is to explain clearly the biblical doctrines of sin and salvation, with appeal to the evidences of sin personally experienced by the satanist.

   In addition to the books cited above, a helpful volume is the classic by B. B. Warfield, *The Plan of Salvation* (repr. Grand Rapids: Eerdmans, 1975).

2. The satanist "religion" of hedonism logically should cause satanists to consider seriously the reality of heaven and hell.

   a. Satanism is the religion of hedonism, or self-indulgence. One could argue with a satanist that if sin and salvation, heaven and hell do exist, the consistent hedonist has every reason to investigate their reality and determine the best way to avoid sin and hell and the best way to enjoy salvation and heaven.

   b. What could be more self-fulfilling and "hedonistic" than eternity in bliss? Satanists owe it to their own philosophy of hedonism to explore the truth claims of Christianity.

   c. A book relating to this kind of argument is John Piper, *Desiring God: Meditations of a Christian Hedonist* (Portland, Oreg.: Multnomah Press, 1986).

3. The satanist worldview cannot account for the reality of sin.

   a. Satanists who deny the reality of sin (and therefore the necessity of salvation) must account for what appears to be sin in the world.

   b. Arguing from a satanist worldview, wouldn't it be "sin" to deny oneself and believe in the gospel? If satanists grant that sin exists (i.e., the sin of denying oneself to believe in the gospel), then Christians can conduct an intelligent discussion on the *nature* of sin rather than the *existence* of sin.

   c. Good introductory doctrine or theology books provide insight into the nature of sin (see the books cited above).

D. The Biblical View of Sin and Salvation

1. Sin is rebellion against God.

   a. Sin is not the invention of man.

   b. Sin is possible when responsible moral agents are given the ability to love God or to rebel against God and his standards.

   c. When people act against God, they are acting in concert with Satan. Jesus described them as belonging "to your father, the devil, and you want to carry out your father's desire. He was a murderer from the beginning, not holding to the truth, for there is no truth in him. When he lies, he speaks his native language, for he is a liar and the father of lies" (John 8:44).

   d. Satanists glory in being accountable to no one or no standard, but the Bible says that such lawlessness is sin (1 John 3:4).

2. The Bible tells us that all humans have sinned, beginning with the first humans and continuing through all the history of mankind (Rom. 5:12–14).

3. There is nothing anyone can do to provide for one's own salvation (Rom. 4:1–6). Salvation comes as the gift of grace (Eph. 2:8–10) through the death of Christ on the cross on our behalf (Rom. 3:23–26).

4. Judgment will come to all humans. Those who have been reconciled to God by Christ will receive eternal life, and those who have rejected the provision for their sins will receive eternal punishment (Matt. 25:46).

5. While rebellious satanists may believe that reconciliation with God is the opposite of what they want, peace with God is the only way to experience true fulfillment, peace, and eternal life.

   Jesus said, "I am the light of the world. Whoever follows me will never walk in darkness, but will have the light of life" (John 8:12), and "I am the resurrection and the life. He who believes in me will live, even though he dies; and whoever lives and believes in me will never die" (John 11:25).

6. Satanists, who reject God's provision for eternal life, have rejected the only way whereby they can truly be fulfilled, happy, at peace, and in possession of the ultimate in human experience.

   The apostle Paul promised, "I consider that our present sufferings are not worth comparing with the glory that will be revealed in us . . . [as we are] brought into the glorious freedom of the children of God" (Rom. 8:18, 21).

Part V:
Witnessing Tips

I. Remember that satanism is not a traditional religion.

A. *Most satanists consider themselves atheistic, so approach them as you would anyone who does not believe in a supreme being.*

  1. Explain that a truly rational person should be willing to examine the evidence for the existence of God.

  2. Focus on arguments for the existence of God that emphasize the theistic foundation for logic and reasoning.

  3. Challenge satanists to justify rationally their own worldview.

B. *The few satanists who acknowledge the existence of God may be afraid they are beyond hope and cannot escape hell.*

  1. Focus on the reality of God, Satan, sin, and hell *but also* the reality of Christ's sacrifice, which can redeem them even if they think they have "sold their souls to the devil."

  2. Remind them that the devil does not control their eternal destiny; God does: "Do not be afraid of those who kill the body but cannot kill the soul. Rather, be afraid of the one who can destroy both soul and body in hell" (Matt. 10:28).

C. *For most teenaged self-taught satanists, satanism is more a symptom of multiple personal problems than a religious rejection or belief.*

  1. Remember that most teenaged satanists use drugs and need successful substance abuse intervention.

  2. Feelings of personal powerlessness and insignificance can propel teenagers toward satanism, so an effective witness should include focus on the life-transforming power of the gospel (Rom. 1:16).

II. Remember that satanism involves self-centeredness, self-indulgence, and self-gratification.

A. *Explain that Christianity is the only path to true self-fulfillment by using Jesus' many paradoxes about "blessed are the meek for they will inherit the earth" (Matt. 5:5), "love your enemies and pray for those who persecute you" (Matt. 5:44), and "whoever finds his life will lose it, and whoever loses his life for my sake will find it" (Matt. 10:39).*

B. *Challenge the hedonistic (self-serving) satanists that the ultimate fulfillment of hedonism is an eternity of bliss, which is only possible by surrender to the Lord Jesus Christ (Matt. 6:33).*

C. *Remind satanists that material gratification in this life is insignificant compared with an eternity under God's judgment: "What good will it be for a man if he gains the whole world, yet forfeits his soul?" (Matt. 16:26).*

III. Remember that satanists misunderstand and mischaracterize Christianity and the Bible.

A. *Challenge satanists regarding their understanding of Christianity.*

1. Ask them to define what they mean by *God, Jesus, sin, salvation*, and so on.

2. Don't merely disagree with their definitions, but challenge them to support the definitions from the Christian worldview in which they are found.

B. *Clarify for satanists what Christianity really teaches.*

1. Define all terms carefully, unambiguously, and clearly.

2. Support your points with clear, contextual Bible passages.

IV. Don't take personal offense at satanists' mockery and rejection of what you know to be the truth.

A. *Show satanists through your well-reasoned discussion and fully supported argumentation that you are a rational, responsible human.*

B. *Challenge satanists to control their mockery unless they can answer all your well-reasoned arguments and also substantiate the truthfulness of their worldview.*

C. *Remember that Jesus acknowledged persecution would follow Christians, but God's grace is sufficient to protect us and give us the necessary boldness to stand for the truth (Matt. 10:21–23).*

Part VI:
Selected Bibliography

I. Primary Sources (Promoting or Sympathetic to Satanism or Occultism)

Barton, Blanche. *The Secret Life of a Satanist: The Authorized Biography of Anton LaVey*. Los Angeles: Feral House, 1990.

Crowley, Aleister. *The Confessions of Aleister Crowley: An Autobiography*. New York: Hill and Wang, 1970.

LaVey, Anton Szandor. *The Satanic Bible*. New York: Avon Books, 1969.

_____. *The Satanic Rituals*. New York: Avon Books, 1972.

_____. *The Compleat Witch, or What to Do When Virtue Fails*. New York: Dodd, Mead, 1970.

Regardie, Israel. *The Eye in the Triangle: An Interpretation of Aleister Crowley*. Phoenix: Falcon Press, 1982.

Wolfe, Burton H. *The Devil's Avenger*. New York: Pyramid, 1974.

II. Secondary Sources—Reference (Sources Not Specifically Christian)

Adler, Margot. *Drawing Down the Moon*. Boston: Beacon Press, 1986.

Ashe, Geoffrey. *Do What You Will: A History of Anti-Morality*. New York: W. H. Allen, 1974.

Boyer, Paul, and Stephen Nissenbaum. *Salem Possessed: The Social Origins of Witchcraft*. Cambridge, Mass.: Harvard University Press, 1974.

Buckland, Raymond. *Buckland's Complete Book of Witchcraft*. St. Paul: Llewellyn, 1990.

Carlson, Shawn, and Gerald Larue, eds. *Satanism in America*. El Cerrito, Calif.: Gaia Press, 1989.

A skeptical view of all supernatural or paranormal reports, including Christianity, but with some useful critical evaluation of contemporary false assumptions about satanism.

Cavendish, Richard. *The Black Arts*. New York: Capricorn, 1968.

A classic source of information on general occultism.

Chancellor, E. Beresford. *The Hell Fire Club*. London: P. Allan, 1925.

Demos, John Putnam. *Entertaining Satan: Witchcraft and the Culture of Early New England*. New York: Oxford University Press, 1982.

Encyclopedia of Occultism and Parapsychology: A Compendium of Information on the Occult Sciences, Magic, Demonology, Superstitions, Spiritism,

Mysticism, Metaphysics, Psychical Science, and Parapsychology, with Biographical . . . Detroit: Gale Research, 1982.

Gokey, Francis X. *The Terminology for the Devil and Evil Spirits in the Apostolic Fathers.* Washington D.C.: Catholic University of America Press, 1961.

Goodman, Felicitas D. *How About Demons: Possession and Exorcism in the Modern World.* Bloomington: Indiana University Press, 1988.

Goran, Morris Herbert. *Fact, Fraud, and Fantasy: The Occult and Pseudo-Sciences.* South Brunswick, N.J.: A. A. Barnes, 1979.

Grant, Kenneth. *Aleister Crowley and the Hidden God.* New York: Samuel Weiser, 1974.

Hansen, Chadwick. *Witchcraft at Salem.* New York: George Braziller, 1969.

Hutton, Ronald. *The Pagan Religions of the Ancient British Isles.* Oxford: Blackwell, 1991.

Kelly, Henry Ansgar. *The Devil, Demonology, and Witchcraft: The Development of Christian Beliefs in Evil Spirits.* Garden City, N.Y.: Doubleday, 1968.

King, Francis. *The Magical World of Aleister Crowley.* London: Weidenfeld and Nicolson, 1977.

Levack, Brian P. *The Witch-Hunt in Early Modern Europe.* New York: Longman, 1987.

Lyons, Arthur. *Satan Wants You: The Cult of Devil Worship in America.* New York: Mysterious Press, 1988.

One of the best short surveys of contemporary American satanism.

Moriarty, Anthony. *The Psychology of Adolescent Satanism.* Westport, Conn.: Praeger, 1992.

Parrinder, Edward Geoffrey. *Witchcraft: European and African.* New York: Barnes & Noble, 1963.

An important evaluation of witchcraft and magic—well-researched, well-reasoned, and well-written—from a premier expert on world religions.

Partner, Peter. *The Murdered Magicians: The Templars and Their Myth.* Rochester, Vt.: Thorsons, 1987.

Rhodes, Henry Taylor Fowkes. *The Satanic Mass.* Secaucus, N.J.: Citadel Press, 1974.

Rose, Elliot. *A Razor for a Goat: A Discussion of Certain Problems in the History of Witchcraft and Diabolism.* Toronto: University of Toronto Press, 1962.

Rudwin, Maximillian J. *The Devil in Legend and Literature.* New York: AMS Press, 1970.

Russell, Jeffrey Burton. *The Devil: Perceptions of Evil from Antiquity to Primitive Christianity.* Ithaca, N.Y.: Cornell University Press, 1977.

The world's leading academic expert on the history of satanism, with books meticulously documented, well-researched, and objectively evaluated.

_____. *Lucifer, the Devil in the Middle Ages.* Ithaca, N.Y.: Cornell University Press, 1984.

_____. *Mephistopheles: The Devil in the Modern World.* Ithaca, N.Y.: Cornell University Press, 1986.

_____. The Prince of Darkness: Radical Evil and the Power of Good in History_. Ithaca, N.Y.: Cornell University Press, 1988.

_____. Satan: The Early Christian Tradition_. Ithaca, N.Y.: Cornell University Press, 1981.

_____. Witchcraft in the Middle Ages_. Ithaca: Cornell University Press, 1972.

St. Clair, David. _Say You Love Satan_. New York: Dell, 1987.

Schutze, Jim. _Cauldron of Blood: The Matamoros Cult Killings_. New York: Avon Books, 1989.

Spence, Lewis. _An Encyclopaedia of Occultism: A Compendium of Information on the Occult Science, Occult Personalities, Psychic Science, Magic, Demonology, Spiritism, Mysticism, and Metaphysics_. New Hyde Park, N.Y.: University Books, 1968.

Symonds, John, and Kenneth Grant, eds. _The Magical Record of the Beast 666: The Diaries of Aleister Crowley (1914–1920)_. Quebec, Canada: Next Step Publications, 1972.

Trevor-Roper, H. R. _The European Witch-Craze of the Sixteenth and Seventeenth Centuries and Other Essays_. New York: Harper & Row, 1967.

Wilson, Colin. _The Occult: A History_. New York: Random House, 1971.

III. Secondary Sources—Christian Reference

Alexander, William Menzies. _Demonic Possession in the New Testament_. Grand Rapids: Baker, 1980.

Brooks, Thomas. _Precious Remedies Against Satan's Devices_. 1652; reprint, Carlisle, Pa.: Banner of Truth Trust, 1990.

Cooper, John Charles. _The Black Mask_. Pleasantville, N.Y.: Fleming H. Revell, 1990.

Dickason, C. Fred. _Demon Possession and the Christian_. Westchester, Ill.: Crossway Books, 1987.

We do not agree with Dickason's assertion that Christians can be controlled against their wills by demonic power.

Green, Michael. _I Believe in Satan's Downfall_. Grand Rapids: Eerdmans, 1981.

Gross, Edward N. _Miracles, Demons, and Spiritual Warfare_. Grand Rapids: Baker, 1990.

One of the best biblical evaluations.

Koch, Kurt. _Between Christ and Satan_. Grand Rapids: Kregel, 1962.

A drawback to Koch's works is his heavy dependence on undocumented personal experience stories.

_____. The Devil's Alphabet_. Grand Rapids: Kregel, 1969.

_____. Satan's Devices_. Grand Rapids: Kregel, 1978.

Martin, Malachi. _Hostage to the Devil_. New York: Bantam Books, 1976.

A Roman Catholic's insightful analysis, although Protestants will have several points of disagreement.

Mayhue, Richard. *Unmasking Satan.* Wheaton, Ill.: Victor Books, 1988.

Parker, Russ. *Battling the Occult.* Downers Grove, Ill.: InterVarsity Press, 1990.

Passantino, Bob and Gretchen Passantino. *When the Devil Dares Your Kids.* Ann Arbor, Mich.: Servant, 1991.

IV. Other Secondary Sources (Not Recommended)

Bass, Ellen, and Laura Davis. *The Courage to Heal.* New York: HarperCollins, 1992.

Friesen, James. *Uncovering the Mystery of MPD.* San Bernardino, Calif.: Here's Life, 1991.

Institoris, Heinrich. *Malleus Maleficarum.* New York: B. Blom, 1970.

One of the many editions available of this early but inaccurate work that provided the fuel for the witch craze of the late Middle Ages. Its unsubstantiated and fanciful depictions of satanic activities, curses, masses, and powers are still used today by the credulous to affirm their belief in a worldwide, bloodthirsty satanic conspiracy.

Johnston, Jerry. *The Edge of Evil.* Dallas: Word, 1989.

Larson, Bob. *Satanism: The Seduction of America's Youth.* Nashville: Thomas Nelson, 1988.

Raschke, Carl A. *Painted Black.* San Francisco: HarperCollins, 1990.

Ryder, Daniel. *Breaking the Circle of Satanic Ritual Abuse.* Minneapolis: Comp-Care, 1992.

Sellers, Sean. *Web of Darkness.* Tulsa: Victory House, 1990.

While Sellers's own story has credibility, his other information on the broader issues of satanism is secondhand and not necessarily reliable.

Smith, Michelle, and Lawrence Pazder. *Michelle Remembers.* New York: Congdon & Lattes, 1980.

Stratford, Lauren. *Satan's Underground.* Eugene, Oreg.: Harvest House, 1988. Reprint, Gretna, La.: Pelican Books, 1990.

————. *Stripped Naked.* Gretna, La.: Pelican Books, 1993.

Terry, Maury. *The Ultimate Evil.* New York: Bantam, 1987.

Warnke, Mike, with Dave Balsiger and Les Jones. *The Satan Seller.* Plainfield, N.J.: Logos International, 1972.

The most popular Christian title on satanism since its publication in 1972, but it is demonstrably untrue. The falsity of the story and the ministry failings of Mike Warnke were exposed and thoroughly documented in the article by Jon Trott and Mike Hertenstein, "Selling Satan," *Cornerstone* 21, no. 98 (June–July 1992): 7–38; and in their subsequent book, *Selling Satan* (Chicago: Cornerstone Press, 1993).

Warnke, Mike. *Schemes of Satan.* Tulsa: Victory House, 1991.

Part VII:
Parallel Comparison Chart

Note: Satanist beliefs are summarized in each instance rather than directly quoted for three reasons: (1) Satanists do not hold anyone's pronouncements as authoritative or binding on all satanists; (2) satanists are not uniform in their beliefs; and (3) satanists by and large ignore most distinctions in biblical theology because of their disdain for the Bible. However, each summary is representative of a significant number of satanists, and the preceding theology section (Part IV) provides whatever direct documentation is available.

Satanists Believe	The Bible Teaches

The Bible

Satanists reject the inspiration and authority of the Bible. (See Part IV, Section II.A–B.)	Hebrews 4:12 warns, "The word of God is living and active. Sharper than any double-edged sword, it penetrates even to dividing soul and spirit, joints and marrow; it judges the thoughts and attitudes of the heart."
	Second Timothy 3:15–17 describes God's Word as "able to make you wise for salvation through faith in Christ Jesus" and "God-breathed and . . . useful for teaching, rebuking, correcting and training in righteousness, so that the man of God may be thoroughly equipped for every good work." (See Part IV, Section II.C–D.)

God

Most satanists reject belief in any supreme being or god, although some believe in a neutral, natural, nonmaterial universal force that they can use for their own power. A few believe in but reject the authority of the God of the Bible. (See Part IV, Section III.A–B, and Part V, Section I.B.)

Romans 1:18–20 declares that all people know that God exists: "The wrath of God is being revealed from heaven against all the godlessness and wickedness of men who suppress the truth by their wickedness, since what may be known about God is plain to them, because God has made it plain to them. For since the creation of the world God's invisible qualities—his eternal power and divine nature—have been clearly seen, being understood from what has been made, so that men are without excuse." (See Part IV, Section III.C–D.)

Jesus Christ

Most satanists do not believe that Jesus Christ is a historical figure, much less that he is God incarnate or our savior. Those who admit to his historical existence view him as a weakling and a failure. (See Part IV, Section IV.A–B.)

Peter affirmed the historicity of Jesus Christ: "We did not follow cleverly invented stories when we told you about the power and coming of our Lord Jesus Christ, but we were eyewitnesses of his majesty" (2 Peter 1:16; see also Luke 1:1–4; Acts 26:25–26). Jesus' power, wisdom, and courage were displayed in his willing self-sacrifice on our behalf, as when he declared, "I lay down my life for the sheep [sinners].... The reason my Father loves me is that I lay down my life—only to take it up again. No one takes it from me, but I lay it down of my own accord. I have authority to lay it down and authority to take it up again" (John 10:15, 17–18). (See Part IV, Section IV.C–D.)

Satan

Satanists worship Satan, whether they ascribe the title to themselves (most common), to some nonmaterial force they use for their own self-gratification (also popular), or to the evil spirit described in the Bible (a few, especially young satanists who grew up in Christian homes). (See Part IV, Section V.A–B, and Part V, Section I.A–C.)

The Bible describes Satan as the chief fallen angel (Luke 10:18), Beelzebul (Matt. 10:25), "the evil one" (Matt. 5:37). Jesus' coming (and death—Col. 2:15) destroyed Satan's power: "I saw Satan fall like lightning from heaven" (Luke 10:18). Satan is called the original liar (John 8:44) and the one who accuses the righteous (Job 1:6–12; Rev. 12:10). He is also referred to as a ruler of this wicked world and evil spiritual forces (Eph. 2:2; 6:12; John 14:30). The ultimate destination of Satan and his demons is the lake of fire (Matt. 25:41; Rev. 20:10). (See Part IV, Section V.C–D.)

Human Beings

Satanists reject the idea that humans are accountable to God, society, or any standard of morals or ethics. Most satanists believe that the majority of humans are ignorant and deserve to be exploited by the satanist elite who are governed by rational self-interest. (See Part IV, Section VI.A–B.)

Humanity was created perfect, sinless, and in God's image: "So God created man in his own image, in the image of God he created him; male and female he created them. God blessed them . . ." (Gen. 1:27–28a). Hebrews 2:14–18 describes the nature of humanity in terms of the perfect humanity of Christ in his incarnation and in contrast to humanity corrupted by sin: "Since the children have flesh and blood, he too shared in their humanity so that by his death he might destroy him who holds the power of death—that is, the devil—and free those who all their lives were held in slavery by their fear of death. For surely it is not angels he helps, but Abraham's descendants. For this reason he had to be made like his brothers in every way, in order that he might become

87

a merciful and faithful high priest in service to God, and that he might make atonement for the sins of the people. Because he himself suffered when he was tempted, he is able to help those who are being tempted." (See Part IV, Section VI.C–D.)

Sin and Salvation

Satanists reject the reality of sin, see no need for salvation, and believe self-fulfillment is accomplished wholly through self-effort. (See Part IV, Section VII.A–B, and Part V, Section II.A–C.)

By Adam and Eve's initial sin, humanity was condemned and made sinful (Rom. 5:12–21). "All have sinned and fall short of the glory of God" (Rom. 3:23), but humanity is not left without redemption, "and are justified freely by his grace through the redemption that came by Christ Jesus" (Rom. 3:24). Jesus Christ is the only way of salvation (Acts 4:12), and he promises, "I am the resurrection and the life. He who believes in me will live, even though he dies; and whoever lives and believes in me will never die" (John 11:25). Those who deny the reality of sin and think that they can be fulfilled through self-effort are condemned: "Woe to those who call evil good and good evil; who put darkness for light and light for darkness; who put bitter for sweet and sweet for bitter! Woe to those who are wise in their own eyes and clever in their own sight." (Isa. 5:20–21). Such people God will send to eternal punishment, but those who are saved by Jesus Christ receive eternal life (Matt. 25:46). (See Part IV, Section VII.C–D.)

Part VIII:
Glossary

I. Terms Exclusive to Satanism

666
"The Mark of the Beast" mentioned in the cryptic book of Revelation (Rev. 13:18). Used symbolically by satanists as identification with the worst of anti-Christianity.

Anti-morality
Term that can refer to a particular popular diversion among some upper-class men in Europe and the British Isles at various times during the seventeenth and eighteenth centuries. These associations, or "clubs," were often called "Hellfire Clubs." The movement was characterized by a disdain for authority, indulgence in sex, alcohol, gambling, and gluttony, and a rejection of Christianity. Much of contemporary satanism can be traced to this kind of philosophy.

Black Mass
A reversal and profaning of the Roman Catholic mass. Once a popular feature of satanism and anti-morality, but less so now since so many people are unfamiliar with Christian ritual. The recitation of the Lord's Prayer backward is still popular, as is desecration of Communion.

FFF
Coded form of the number of "the Beast" of Revelation 13 (666). F is the sixth letter of the alphabet.

Grotto
Term used by some satanists to signify their worship group, synonymous to a witches' coven. Other satanists use "coven"; some use "church."

Nema Natas
"Satan Amen" backward, one of the most common satanic cryptic messages. Writing backward is one magical tool of satanism as well as being an elementary code.

Satan
Hebrew for "Adversary," the angel Lucifer who rebelled against God and became the chief of the demons (other angels who sinned). Satanists worship Satan, although they might have different beliefs about his identity. Many satanists have no belief in the supernatural and worship themselves, calling themselves "Satan" in opposition to what they perceive as the self-denial and abasement of Christianity. Some satanists believe in some sort of intangible power or force that can be harnessed for personal gain and personify that force as "Satan." Others don't know if a spirit being exists named Satan, but they are convinced that "calling on" or "worshiping" Satan produces results.

Satanism	Any religious system incorporating the worship of Satan, whatever Satan is conceived to be (the self, self-indulgence, evil, evil principles, myth, demon, or deity).
Set, Temple of	One of the public satanic churches, founded by Michael Aquino, who used to be an important member of the Church of Satan. Aquino's brand of satanism is modeled after Egyptian religion and affirms a belief in malevolent spiritual forces.
Unholy kiss	In satanism, the kiss of allegiance to Satan, usually done by kissing the buttocks of the figure representing Satan.

II. Terms Used in Satanism and Other Religious Systems (Often Including Witchcraft)

All Hallow's Eve	Halloween, the day (evening) before "All Saints' Day" (November 1), which corresponds to the pagan holiday of Samhain, the "day of the dead" midway between the fall equinox and winter solstice.
Altar	Any flat surface used for religious rites and for any arrangement of ritual tools or other items. Most religions have altars, including certain Christian denominations (patterned after the altar of the Old Testament temple), witchcraft, and satanism.
Amulet	Any object said to possess power to bring good luck or to ward against bad luck.
Arcane	Secret, esoteric, or mysterious.
August Eve	July 31, called Lughnasadh, one of the four great festivals celebrated by witches, satanists, and other occultists.
Baphomet	The goat-headed god of sexual indulgence and physical gratification; the trump card in the Tarot deck; common symbol of satanism, sometimes used in witchcraft.
Beltane	One of the major Celtic festivals celebrated on May Day (May 1), occurring between the spring equinox and the summer solstice, named after the sun god of flocks and the underworld. The day before is called Walpurgisnacht and is said to be when the underworld and the world of the living can communicate freely.
Bind	In magic, to restrain through the use of magic.
Black book	See *Book of Shadows*.
Black magic	Destructive magic, or that magic directed against someone else. While some people try to distinguish qualitatively between black magic and white magic, there is no qualitative difference. Both

90

attempt to shape reality through the power of the will, usually through manipulation of supposed "psychic" powers.

Blood ritual Most common in satanism, although also in various folk religions. Blood symbolizes life and power; consequently blood is used in rituals of power and life. LaVey says using blood in a ritual is the amateur's way of achieving power, but that the mature satanist needs no "prop" like blood.

Book of Shadows The "black book," or personal workbook, of a witch or satanist, the collection of spells, rituals, and journaled experiences unique to each, usually including traditions received from other practitioners. Also called the "grimoire."

Cernunnos The ancient Celtic version of the "horned god," equal to the collective spirit of the animal world.

Chalice A sacred ceremonial cup, used in witchcraft to symbolize the element of water, and in satanism for the desecrated Communion drink (sometimes stolen Communion wine, urine, blood, or other substances).

Charm Magical words or an object associated with magical power.

Coven Common term to describe a group of witches who share a common witchcraft tradition and work magic and worship ritually together. Usually the group numbers thirteen or fewer. Some self-taught satanists call their groups covens as well, although today the term is usually restricted to witches. See *Grotto*.

Coven sword The ritual sword used symbolically in a particular coven's rituals.

Curse The use of magic to harm someone or something.

Equinox, spring The dates when the amount of light and darkness in one twenty-
Equinox, fall four hour period is approximately the same (caused by the sun crossing the celestial equator). Important holidays in both witchcraft and satanism.

Evocation The magic rite of calling power out from the practitioner.

Familiar An animal with whom the magical practitioner feels a psychic affinity.

Goat of Mendes Also called Baphomet, the goat-headed god popularized by the Knights Templar and now common to witchcraft and satanism. Described and used differently in witchcraft than in satanism.

God In witchcraft, the male aspect of divine or spiritual reality; the male aspect of life; usually the consort of the goddess in ritual worship. In satanism, Satan, as a being to be worshiped; the Christian God, as a being to be blasphemed. Most satanists have

91

	no belief in a transcendent, all-powerful, infinite God as he is described in the Bible.
Grimoire	See *Book of Shadows*.
Halloween	All Hallow's Eve, the day before All Saints' Day, corresponding to the pagan holiday of Samhain.
Incantation	A rhyming or repetitive chant used for the purpose of casting a magical spell.
Incubus	A (demonic) spirit having intercourse with a woman.
Invoke	To magically call something in (usually to the ritual site) from without.
Lammas Day	A witchcraft and satanic holiday corresponding to Lughnasadh.
Left-hand path	Term for destructive occultism and satanism used by "white magic" practitioners, who practice magic only for healing or help rather than for cursing or hurting.
Lughnasadh	August 1, a "Grand Sabbat," one of the four great feast days in witchcraft and satanism.
Magic	Often spelled "magick" by its practitioners to distinguish it from stage magic or sleight of hand; the supposed ability to use rituals, spells, thoughts, and spiritual power to affect the material world.
Magick circle	In witchcraft, the psychic circle corresponding in plane dimensions to the circle drawn on the ground or floor; used as a focus of power to allow communication or passage through different dimensions. Satanists often speak of the magick circle as well, meaning the same, and also trace it around a sacrifice site, or (as a warning to enemies) around something associated with or belonging to an enemy.
Necromancy	Divination associated with the dead; supposed communication with the dead.
Necrophilia	Having sexual intercourse with a corpse.
Ormelc, Feast of	Also spelled Oimelc; in witchcraft, one of the eight annual festivals, celebrated on February 1 or 2; also called Candlemas.
Ouiji board	Produced as a game by Parker Brothers, taken from a nineteenth-century form of divination using an alphabet board and a "pointer" supposedly manipulated by psychic power to spell out psychic messages.
Pentacle	The five-pointed star surrounded by a circle or ring.
Pentagram	The five-pointed star, a common symbol of witchcraft (with one point at the top) and satanism (with one point at the bottom).

Phallic symbol   A symbol of the penis, common in magic and ritual in witch-craft, satanism, and many folk religions.

Potion   Any liquid herbal concoction used for healing or harming in conjunction with the practice of magic.

Sabbat   One of the eight annual festivals of witchcraft and satanism; four correspond to the solstices and equinoxes, and four (called Grand Sabbats) occur midway between the solstices and equinoxes.

Samhain   The most important witchcraft and satanist holiday, corre-sponding to the Christian All Hallow's Eve and All Saints' Day (November 1); the Celtic festival of the dead.

Seal of Solomon   The Star of David, two interlocking, equilateral triangles, used in witchcraft and satanism, symbol of the Order of the Golden Dawn, an old occult society.

Solstice, summer   One of the eight great witchcraft and satanism festivals, occur-ring on June 21, corresponding to the Christian celebration of St. John's Day.

Solstice, winter   One of the eight great witchcraft and satanism festivals, occur-ring on December 21, corresponding to the Christian celebra-tion of Christmas.

Sorcery   The magical manipulation of nonphysical forces to affect the physical world or other people.

Spiritism   The practice of communicating with the dead, usually through the use of a "medium" or human go-between (in the New Age called a "channeler").

Succubus   A spirit having intercourse with a man.

Talisman   An object like a charm or amulet, except that it is manufactured; said to embody magical power, especially for good luck or pro-tection.

Thaumaturge   The use of magic on people, places, or events outside the practi-tioner himself or herself.

Vampire   In the occult genre, a dead person who comes in spirit or magi-cal form to destroy living persons by drinking their blood.

Walpurgisnacht   See *Beltane*.

Warlock   Originally used to refer to a witch who betrayed fellow witches to the ecclesiastical authorities; erroneously used to refer to male witches. Sometimes self-styled witches, male or female, use the term to refer to themselves.

White magic   Constructive magic, or that magic directed in healing or help-ing. See further under *Black magic*.

93

III. Terms Used in Christianity

All Saints' Day November 1, in the Christian calendar a celebration remembering all Christians who have suffered and died for their faith (martyrs) or who are specially honored for their service in the name of Christ. All Saints' Day is celebrated on the pagan holiday of the dead (see All Hallow's Eve).

Antichrist First John in the Bible describes an "antichrist" as anyone who denies that Jesus is the Christ—in other words, anyone who denies the Christian faith. From other allusions to similar figures in other Scriptures, some biblical interpreters say there will be one great Antichrist immediately before the Second Coming who will epitomize anti-Christianity and enforce his blasphemy throughout the world.

Blasphemer Someone who curses, denounces, or profanes God.

Demon Evil spirit, created as an angel by God but fallen through personal sin.

Demon possession, or Demonization, or Being demonized
To be controlled against one's will by a demon.

Exorcism The Christian ritual of releasing a demonized person from demonic control.

Heresy Literally, a teaching or belief that contradicts what is accepted. A heresy against Christianity, for example, is a teaching or belief that contradicts the central, clear teaching of the Bible as sustained by the Christian church through the centuries.

Idol According to Christianity, any physical representation of a false god. No physical representation is possible of the Christian God, who is spirit, infinite, and omnipresent.

Monotheism Belief in only one true God. Judaism, Islam, and Christianity are the three major monotheistic world religions.

IV. Non-Religious Terms

Backward masking In the recording industry, the practice of laying one track of a record or CD backward. Usually done as a promotional gimmick; said by some to be a method of passing evil or harmful ideas to innocent listeners through their subconscious. There is no scientific evidence that backward masking can persuade someone to believe something.

Cryptic Coded, symbolic, or hidden communication.

Dungeons and Dragons

A fantasy role-playing game using characters patterned after myriad gods, goddesses, and mythological figures; the game requires careful study, intelligence, and dedication. The game and others like it have been accused of compelling teenagers to suicide or other violence. While such a connection has not been proved, the potentially destructive, magical orientation of the game appeals to teenagers vulnerable in that aspect of their lives.

Fantasy role-playing game

Any number of games, most patterned after Dungeons and Dragons, with an elaborate mythological or supernatural world, a heavy dependence on magic and ritual, and requiring intelligence, commitment, and study to play successfully.

Head banging

A common practice among some heavy-metal music fans, consisting of flinging one's head back and forth violently in beat with the music. Sometimes people will actually bang the head against the wall, floor, stage, or speaker. Some critics associate head banging with the effects of occult-themed rock lyrics.

Heavy metal

A form of rock music characterized by discordant, high-decibel, innovative, and chaotic music with lyrics generally celebrating decadence, sexual indulgence, drug use, and self-gratification.

Multiple Personality Disorder (MPD)

A psychiatric designation referring to the rare phenomenon wherein an individual copes with a traumatic event or experience by "splitting" or "fragmenting" corresponding "personalities" (or parts of personalities) while the "core" personality represses the traumatic memory. Responsible experts in dissociative disorder agree that MPD is greatly overdiagnosed today.

Myth

A traditional story (whether true or not) that appeals to the values or worldview of a group by embodying its cultural ideals, deep emotions, and convictions.

Occult

Literally, hidden or secret knowledge; usually refers to any of a number of magical, ritualized practices commonly associated with psychic phenomena in opposition to historic Christianity and biblical revelation.

Pantheism

Literally, "all is God"; the religious worldview that sees all of reality (material or immaterial) as divine: God is everything, everything is God.

Polytheism

Belief in more than one god or many gods.

Sado-masochism

A complex of behavior between individuals who receive sexual pleasure through either giving or receiving pain.

Subliminal message
A visual or audio message indiscernible to the conscious mind, incorporated into a visible or audible message. There is no scientific evidence that this practice has any persuasive ability other than the recipient's self-fulfilling belief that it will work.

Superstition
Term used to refer either to a religious or magical belief held in the face of contrary evidence; or to a belief contrary to what is accepted within the group.

Urban myth
A contemporary story in general circulation with the following characteristics: (1) the story teller usually claims to have personal knowledge of the event ("It happened to my mother," "It happened in the town where my cousin lives," etc.); (2) the story appears to be true, although incredible; (3) the story validates a commonly held, but unverifiable belief; and (4) no evidence or documentation can be adduced to prove the belief.